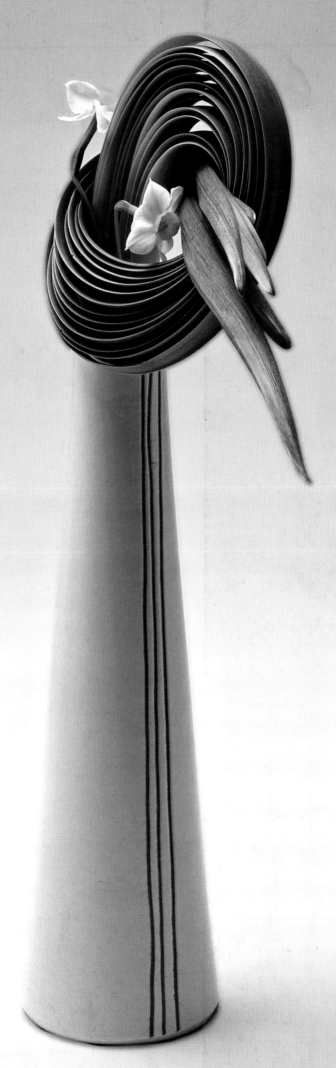

IKEBANA

THE ART OF ARRANGING FLOWERS

SHOZO SATO

foreword by KASEN YOSHIMURA

TUTTLE Publishing

Tokyo | Rutland, Vermont | Singapore

This book is dedicated to the memory of countless past Ikebana masters, who, while striving for perfection, built the foundation on which the art rests today; and to the teachers of Ikebana today, who will mentor a new generation of Ikebana artists for tomorrow.

Published by Tuttle Publishing, an imprint of Periplus Editions (HK) Ltd.

www.tuttlepublishing.com

Copyright © 2008 Shozo Sato

ISBN: 978-4-8053-0943-8 hc
ISBN: 978-4-8053-1266-7 pb

Distributed by:
North America, Latin America & Europe
Tuttle Publishing
364 Innovation Drive
North Clarendon, VT 05759-9436 U.S.A.
Tel: 1 (802) 773-8930
Fax: 1 (802) 773-6993
info@tuttlepublishing.com
www.tuttlepublishing.com

Japan
Tuttle Publishing
Yaekari Building, 3rd Floor
5-4-12 Osaki
Shinagawa-ku
Tokyo 141-0032
Tel: (81) 3 5437-0171
Fax: (81) 3 5437-0755
sales@tuttle.co.jp
www.tuttle.co.jp

Asia Pacific
Berkeley Books Pte. Ltd.
61 Tai Seng Avenue, #02-12
Singapore 534167
Tel: (65) 6280-1330
Fax: (65) 6280-6290
inquiries@periplus.com.sg
www.periplus.com

hc 12 11 10 09 08   10 9 8 7 6 5 4 3 2
pb 15 14 13 12   10 9 8 7 6 5 4 3 2 1

Printed in Hong Kong   1211EP

TUTTLE PUBLISHING® is a registered trademark of Tuttle Publishing, a division of Periplus Editions (HK) Ltd.

Page 1: **Freestyle arrangement.** Japanese narcissus.
Vase: Contemporary ceramic.
Page 2: **Freestyle arrangement.** Spirea, larkspur, and anemones.
Vase: Contemporary blue-gazed suiban.
Pages 4–5: A print showing geishas viewing a Rikka arrangement (from the *Seiro-Bijin-Aisugata-Kagami*).
Page 6: **Moribana arrangement.** Vase: Contemporary ceramic
Page 8: **Seika: Informal arrangement in Sanshu Ike.** Vase: Suiban in cast bronze.
Page 10: **Freestyle arrangement.** Vase: Contemporary glass.
Page 14: **Rikka arrangement in the style of Fukyu no Shin**
Page 34: **Seika: Tobi Nejime style Nishu Ike.** Vase: Ceramic suiban
Pages 136–37: **Moribana in the formal basic style.** Vase: Ryusei School suiban in a dark-blue glaze.
Pages 158–59: **Moribana in the semiformal left-hand pattern, basic style.** Vase: Contemporary *suiban* with a dark-blue glaze.

Contents

Foreword

In my opinion, Mr. Shozo Sato is among the very few who have successfully disseminated, in-depth, the traditional arts of Japan to an international audience. To Ikebana we can add the tea ceremony, calligraphy, sumi-e, and kabuki. In Japan, during his youth, Mr. Sato studied Ikebana, ranging from classic to contemporary, and his skill as an artist was clearly evident in his work. Some fifty years have passed since he informed me that he hoped to move to the United States and make a career of disseminating Japanese culture.

My personal thought at the time was that the Japanese world of art would be losing a significant and creative artist. I was concerned about whether he would succeed at such a challenging enterprise. However, once he began teaching at the University of Illinois, it was as if "a fish had returned to familiar waters," and his many activities met with great success. To my great surprise, my earlier concerns were totally unfounded. Through his great persistence and efforts, he established the original Japan House at the University of Illinois; subsequently, many organizations assisted and supported the building of the new Japan House. The Japan House functions as a Japanese cultural center for the student body at the university and for the community at large.

The seemingly endless number and variety of activities Mr. Sato has undertaken to introduce the aesthetics of Japanese culture to the West constitute a great and meritorious achievement. Speaking with experience as the grandmaster of an Ikebana school, it is clear to me that his skill goes beyond thoroughly mastering the craft and technique of Ikebana, which he has done, to a deep understanding of the "soul of the art form." His high level of skill accounts for his success as a teacher and interpreter of Japanese artforms. One of Mr. Sato's earliest contributions was *The Art of Arranging Flowers: A Complete Guide to Japanese Ikebana*, published by Harry N. Abrams, Inc. (1966), which was the first authoritative book in English on Ikebana. It was his dedicated and sincere enthusiasm for disseminating Japanese culture to the world that brought the publication to fruition.

Already some forty years have passed since the publication of that first book, *The Art of Arranging Flowers*. In this new book, the arrangements have been rephotographed in full color, and the entire contents have been updated. The history of Ikebana from its beginning to contemporary times has been included. To have such a book published in English is a celebratory occasion for the world of Japanese Ikebana.

I am confident that experienced and novice Ikebana artists, as well as those simply interested in the art form, will find Mr. Sato's new book enjoyable, informative, and an inspiration for their individual creativity.

Kasen Yoshimura
Third Generation Grandmaster
Ryusei School of Ikebana

Preface

There is a national ceremony in Japan for young men and women who reach the age of twenty-one, to celebrate their entrance to adulthood. When I turned twenty-one, I contemplated how I could commemorate this event and came up with the idea of writing a book to introduce Ikebana to Westerners, which was eventually published as an earlier version of the present volume.

More than forty years have passed since the publication of my first book on Ikebana. Compared to the many centuries that the history of Ikebana covers, forty years is but a brief interval, yet much has taken place in the world of Ikebana since the publication of that first book. The fundamentals of Ikebana are as relevant today as they were then, but many exciting changes and new directions have arisen in this unique form of creativity. When Tuttle Publishing offered to publish a new edition of this book, it gave me the opportunity to update the work and include new trends.

In 2007, Ikebana International, Chapter I, of Washington, D.C., celebrated their fiftieth anniversary, along with many other chapters. Forty years ago, Ikebana International was still a newly established organization, but since that time chapters have spread worldwide, beyond the boundaries of the United States and Europe.

During these intervening forty years, Ikebana has continued to be a vibrant and inspiring art form in Japan, fostering new movements in creativity. The Ryusei School of Ikebana, headquartered in Tokyo, whose tenets form the basis for this book, celebrated its 120th anniversary in 2006. Exhibitions commemorating this anniversary were held across Japan during the summer of 2006. Attendance for these exhibitions exceeded all expectations; the show in Tokyo alone attracted over 30,000 attendees.

The Japanese art of flower arrangement has been described as being at once more subtle, more sensitive, and more sophisticated than the methods of arranging flowers usually employed in other cultures. This is so because Ikebana is an art in Japan in the same sense that painting and sculpture are arts elsewhere. It has a recorded history, it has undergone a coherent development, it has a technical discipline, it is backed by articulate theories, and it has remained a vital medium for creative expression. The greatest creations in this field, to be sure, are apt to be made by the most highly skilled experts, but, just as in painting and sculpture, there is room aplenty for amateurs. Indeed, as this book will show, almost anyone with a little time and inclination can acquire sufficient skills to make beautiful arrangements.

In all of the traditional arts of Japan, the work of the many generations of great masters has developed a foundation that we call classic. This long history continues to be revered in the various disciplines and still serves as a basis for creating new genres of artistic expression. As in other arts, it is necessary to master certain fundamental techniques before proceeding to free creation, since, if these basics are not mastered, success is unlikely.

This book provides readers with a complete introduction to Ikebana—from classic to contemporary styles—and begins with the historical development of Ikebana and its place in Japanese culture. An illustrated survey of the five principal styles—Rikka, Seika, Nageire, Moribana and Free—along with their most important variations, gives readers a firm foundation in Ikebana techniques. For each of the classical styles there is a section on the contemporary version, for all five styles are still in wide use today, although the elaborate Rikka is rarely seen except in exhibitions. In the late 1800s the Ryusei School branched out from the Ikenobo School, which is recognized as the originator of Ikebana and is the oldest existing school. Only the Ryusei and Ikenobo Schools teach Rikka and Seika. All other Ikebana schools teach various styles in modern arrangements.

In addition to revivals and reinterpretations of classic styles such as Rikka and Seika, the reader will be introduced to contemporary Ikebana, which is based upon a foundation in Moribana, or freestyle. The reader will also find illustrated and detailed instructions concerning the selection and preparation of materials, a practical course in the fundamental techniques of Moribana, and suggestions for the many possibilities that open up to those who have mastered the basic lessons.

The developments in contemporary Ikebana compose the largest addition to the original edition, since this is where the greatest advances have been made in the last four decades. I hope that the groundbreaking contemporary arrangements included in this book will inspire you to strive for new heights in creativity in Ikebana for the twenty-first century.

Shōzō Satō

The Japanese and Nature

When branches, flowers, and grasses are cut, they must be put in water to make them last longer. This basic understanding—that plants need water to be sustained—was recognized centuries ago. Therein lies the beginning of Ikebana art.

The islands of Japan are blessed with being located in a temperate zone, with rainfall ranging from moderate to heavy. There are four distinct seasons, and the mountainous terrain is covered with forests that generally are verdantly green, with an abundance of flowers in season. The love of nature is intrinsic to the Japanese culture.

From the earliest times, Japanese homes were open to nature. During the Heian period (eighth to twelfth centuries) the nobility and ruling classes lived in palatial homes that were architecturally classified as *shinden zukuri*. A characteristic of shinden zukuri is that the rooms were arranged around a courtyard: a three- or four-sided enclosure with the rooms facing toward it. Sliding doors separated the rooms, but the walls that faced the courtyard could be lifted up, opening the room out to the veranda and the garden beyond. This feature created the feeling of being out of doors in any part of the home. The enclosed garden was designed to re-create the grandeur of nature, with miniature mountains, waterfalls, lakes, and islands. Most often, the natural views beyond the garden boundaries were incorporated as part of the design.

Shinto, the indigenous religion, has often been called nature worship because all things are deified, and the object and spirit are inseparable. Buddhism, which was introduced during the seventh century, is fundamentally based upon the "laws of nature," and philosophically it is very compatible with Shinto. The two religions have long coexisted, often blending and overlapping. The philosophical basis for both Shinto and Buddhism is the ephemeral nature of all life.

The abundant living plants that manifest the cycle of life have inspired these two sayings, which are ingrained in the Japanese psyche: "When life is created, death will come" and "When form is created, eventually it goes back to dust." Instead of eternity, *mujo*—the teaching that nothing is maintained as you expect and that all is ephemeral—is the core belief of Buddhist philosophy. This belief is the foundation for the Ikebana artist. When the Ikebana artist completes the artwork, at that very moment the art will have completed its mission, and it dies away within a few hours or days. The beauty of Ikebana art is short-lived. The sharp senses of each creative Ikebana artist are dedicated to creating designs that will make plants even more beautiful than in their natural form. This ephemeral beauty, which is the fundamental aspect of Ikebana, touches the viewer's heart. This is especially so in the Seika style of Ikebana.

Sentiment and emotions have always played an important role in all of the arts. This is certainly so in Japan, where the mere mention of a flower's name is often enough to evoke a whole series of ideas, images, and meanings from classical poetry. A cherry blossom is not merely a beautiful flower—it is also a symbol of manliness and bravery. It blossoms briefly but gloriously, then falls quickly before it has withered. The grasses of autumn suggest the nostalgia of a fading summer and the passage of time. For the symbolism associated with a specific plant, see "The Symbolism of Plants," pages 198–204.

To the great majority of Japanese, each flower evokes a particular month of the year and the feelings and memories appropriate to that month. Ikebana arrangements, accordingly, are expected not only to establish a link between man and nature but also to create a mood or atmosphere appropriate to the season, and even to the occasion—a tradition in keeping with the Japanese focus on the ephemeral nature of life, as well. Thus, Ikebana artists typically use floral materials that are in season and change them accordingly. In classical flower arrangements, several different types of plants are used in a single arrangement, to give prominence not only to blossoms but to leaves and flowerless branches as well. Even when a single type of flower is used, an attempt is made to bring out its full implications as a symbol of nature.

Opposite: **A nineteenth-century woodblock print by the Japanese master Hokusai showing figures admiring Kirifuri Falls.**

PART I

Ikebana Through the Centuries

During the earliest times, floral materials were probably placed in a container and rested on the rim of the vase, as an offering at Buddhist altars. This eventually led to the category of *tate hana*, literally meaning "standing flower." Floral materials were arranged to stand upright as in nature, just as a tree grows from the ground.

Simple floral arrangements were made as early as the seventh century, when Buddhism was introduced to Japan from Korea and China. It was the custom at Buddhist monasteries to place flowers before images of the Buddha, and over the centuries these floral offerings acquired a fairly elaborate form. It is thought that when a fifty-three-foot statue of the Buddha was dedicated at the Tōdai-ji monastery in 752 CE, the floral offerings were of immense size and scale. Actual records state that when the monastery was rededicated in the seventeenth century, the floral arrangements before the statue were forty feet high.

Exactly how flowers were arranged before the Buddhist icons in early times is unknown, but later evidence suggests that the typical arrangement consisted of a number of flowers or branches placed artlessly in a tall narrow-necked vase. Sometimes, it appears, stemless blossoms were floated in a shallow bowl or basin. Early statues and tapestries show Buddhist deities holding similar vases, each containing a lotus blossom and leaf. The lotus is a symbol of the universe in Buddhism, so it is likely that the flower was frequently used in early Buddhism.

There is no way of knowing just when flowers began to be used for nonreligious purposes. During Heian times (eighth to twelfth centuries), it was a common custom to send poetry attached to a flowering branch as an expression of admiration and sentiment. This gift was often put in a jar of water and placed in some special place in the room. It is likely that these sentimental sprays of blossoms became the first secular flower arrangements.

From the close of the Heian period to the Kamakura period, in the thirteenth century, a long board lying flat against the wall began to appear as a decorative feature in residences of the court nobility and high-ranking warriors. On this board were placed three low tables, which held accessories ranging from three to five in number. The center table held a candle stand, incense burner, incense holder, and flower vase, and the two side tables held flower arrangements. Flowers were arranged to be one and one-half times the height of the vase, which, compared to arrangements today, is short. On the wall above the tables would be a set of either three or five wall hangings. These formal arrangements were the forerunners of the recessed alcove called the *tokonoma*.

THE TOKONOMA

In the fourteenth and fifteenth centuries, Japanese warriors, who were originally the palace guards, gained power and rose to establish the samurai class, eventually becoming feudal lords. Ikebana, the tea ceremony, calligraphy, composing poetry, and so on, were a vital part of *bun bu* (*bun* means "literary"; *bu* means "military arts"), the training for samurai. Ikebana occupied an important place in the study of the laws of nature, beauty, and the value of life. The shogun became the most powerful of the samurai class, and the shogunate type of government called the *bakufu* was established. These changes brought about alterations in architectural styles. As feudal lords gained stature and supremacy, they wished to display their wealth and power. The first tokonoma was built,

Opposite: **Rikka: Hidari Nagashi** (*hidari* means "left"; *nagashi* means "stream"). Vase: Classic bronze.

Below: A *tokonoma* and built-in shelves in a room at the Sakurai family house of Matsue. A treasured art object—a lacquer box—and an incense burner are placed on the shelves. Another *tokonoma*, decorated with an arrangement, can be seen in a second room to the left. (Photo: Tokio Yamanouchi)

no doubt, to display suits of armor, but once the unification of the nation was established and peaceful times arrived, art objects, rather than armor, were displayed in the tokonoma. One entire side of the main room—the tokonoma—was reserved as important space for displaying and appreciating fine arts, serving as a "picture frame" for the central focus.

The tokonoma is considered an important feature of the *shoin zukuri* style, which, like the shinden zukuri discussed earlier, is considered one of the two great styles in premodern Japanese residential architecture. The shoin zukuri style developed among the warrior classes. Its major feature was the use of sliding doors to open a room up to the veranda, instead of a wall that lifted up. The shoin house featured the tokonoma and a built-in desk and/or built-in shelves.

The size and design of the tokonoma varied, but in the typical dwelling it was about six feet wide by three feet deep.

The floor of the tokonoma was raised several inches higher than that of the room. It was customary to decorate the tokonoma with a group of items: often a hanging scroll, decorated with a painting or calligraphy, and a flower arrangement. A treasured art object of some sort was usually placed on an adjoining shelf. These were the only ornaments, save possibly the paintings on the door and wall panels, and they served as a focal point in the room, since there were very few other furnishings.

The very prominence of the tokonoma necessitated that the decorations be as interesting and of as high a quality as possible. The objects, including the floral arrangements, were changed periodically to reflect the season. Although a floral arrangement offered the greatest flexibility in design, it was important to coordinate the arrangement with the season and the other art objects in the tokonoma.

Opposite: **A Rikka of Japanese iris arrangement.** Vase: Bronze Period Rikka. This arrangement is an inspired replication of a traditional Rikka from the fifteenth and sixteenth centuries. This style arrangement is based upon the use of one category of plant material. This bountiful display of Japanese iris, whose habitat is in or near the water, evokes the refreshing coolness of early summer. Generally speaking, in such an arrangement as this, plants that are known for growing by the water are not combined with plants that grow on dry land. However, there is room for flexibility, and a stem of variegated Japanese pampas grass provides, in the center right-hand position, a sweeping line for *mikoshi*, a division in the composition that symbolically represents mist separating the sacred from the common. The pampas also expresses refreshing coolness. Japanese iris can be used in arrangements in all seasons, but this one, which expresses great abundance of summer, is clearly a summer arrangement. For contrasts in color, the yellowing blades of iris leaves are used behind the *sho shin* (center of Rikka). A species of yellow water lilies in the lower part gives a nice accent.

The floors of traditional homes are covered with tatami mats. The size of each mat is six by three feet, with a thickness of two inches. Originally, the tatami mat was used as a bed, and a half-size version served as a cushion or seat. Homes in the shinden or shoin zukuri style had floors of highly polished wood. Eventually, tatami covered the floors of the entire house. The tatami size became a fundamental measuring system.

The interior space of traditional Japanese rooms, generally speaking, consists of straight lines, rectangular surfaces, and relatively neutral colors. For example, the size of the *fusuma*, or sliding doors, is based on the tatami mat, which measures three by six feet. For all traditional homes, the standard floor-to-ceiling measurement for a small room is nine to twelve feet. These proportions are also used in Ikebana, and the natural curves of floral materials provide a beautiful contrast to the stark simplicity of the straight architectural lines.

RIKKA: THE EARLIEST STYLE

Ultimately, the early Buddhist floral decorations were intended to symbolize the idealized beauty of paradise, and as a result they were generally both ornate and sumptuous. The same attributes were preserved in Rikka—the first Ikebana style—which aimed not so much at revealing the beauty of flowers as at using flowers to embody an elevated concept of the cosmos. A Rikka arrangement can be interpreted on a number of different philosophical levels, but it invariably has within it a striving for something that transcends the natural world. Paradoxically, this means that it has a man-made look, for only man conceives of otherworldly beauty.

A number of scroll paintings from the Heian and Kamakura periods (704–1186 and 1185–1333 CE) show floral arrangements placed before Buddhist images. One of the more amusing examples is in the scroll known as the *Frolic of the Animals (Choju Giga)*, which dates from the eleventh or possibly twelfth century, and which irreverently portrays a frog sitting like a Buddha and monkeys as priests. As in many other examples, the arrangement consists of a tall lotus flower flanked by two shorter lotus buds. The three-part arrangement recalls the customary placement of the Buddhist altar triad, with a Buddha in the middle and a smaller attendant on each side.

The picture scrolls show many floral offerings of the types known as *mitsu-gusoku* and *go-gosoku*, or three-article arrangements and five-article arrangements. The three-article arrangement consisted of an incense burner with a candlestick on one side of it and a vase of flowers on the other side. When Rikka took form, it retained the three-vase arrangement, harking back to the Buddhist three-image group. This is still

Above, left: **The sons of a samurai receive instruction in the art of flower arranging from a priest. From Nageire Hana Densho, 1684.**

Left: **This woodblock print from the Edo period (1615–1868) depicts an Ikebana exhibit held in the courtyard of a *shinden zukuri* house.**

Bottom, left: This three-article arrangement, probably intended for a home rather than a temple, consists of an incense burner and container, a candle-holder, and a flower arrangement. It is flanked by additional arrangements. The ideogram in the center means "main Buddha," and those on either side "attendant paintings." This illustration is from the *Sendensho*, the earliest book on flower arranging.

Bottom, right: A five-article arrangement placed before three hanging scrolls. The vase at the very center is not an intrinsic part of the group.

Bottom: A *tokonoma* in the late fifteenth or early sixteenth century. The two woodblock prints are part of a single scene. Two Rikka arrangements flank an elaborate stand, which holds an incense burner and has a small third arrangement beneath it.

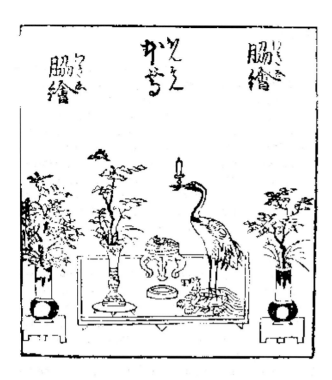

THE OLDEST BOOK ON IKEBANA

Japanese sources trace the origin of Ikebana (*ike* means "to arrange" or "put" and can also mean "alive"; *bana* or *hana* means "flowers") to the time of the eighth Ashikaga shogun, Yoshimasa (1435–1490), a great patron of Zen Buddhism and the arts associated with it. By Yoshimasa's time, however, flower arranging must have been a fairly highly developed art, for the *Sendensho*, the oldest book on the subject, is dated 1445. This short treatise gives comparatively detailed instruction for arrangements to be used on various occasions, such as annual festivals and the celebrations held to commemorate a man's coming of age, entering the priesthood, or taking a wife. Already, it will be seen, the idea that the arrangement should complement the season or event was firmly entrenched. The *Sendensho* is not a continuous narrative, but a series of brief rules and explanations, explaining, among other things, which flowers should be used for various specific purposes, how the vase should be placed, which flowers and combinations of branches are to be avoided, and how to deal with flowers for a tea ceremony. It mentions only two technical words for the components of a flower arrangement: *shin*, or main branch, and *soe-mono*, accompanying or secondary branches. The book is of such a general nature that the lack of other terms does not necessarily mean that none existed, but it seems likely that the branches had not yet been given the more particularized names they were later to acquire.

At the end of the *Sendensho*, there is a notation that the book, having been transmitted to one Fuami in 1445, later passed through several hands, and in 1536 was owned by a man named Senji. This Senji is thought to be identical with the flower master Ikenobo Senno, whose surname, Ikenobo, is the greatest name in the history of Japanese flower arranging.

The Ikenobo "family," which was in reality a succession of priests and flower artists, traces its origins back to the year 621, when Ono-no Imoko, famous as one of Prince Shotoku's first envoys to China, assumed the priestly name Semmu and took up residence at a small temple by a pond, in what was later to become Kyoto. The proper name of the temple was Rokkaku-do, but Semmu's hermitage became known as Ikenobo, which means literally "priest's residence by a pond." The resident priests who followed used the word *sen* in their names: hence Ikenobo Senno was the recipient of the *Sendensho*. Because the names are similar, sometimes having the same pronunciation but written with a different ideogram, a numerical sequence was adopted for the succession of the Ikenobo masters. Hence it was Ikenobo Senko XXXII who was summoned to the Imperial Palace in 1629 to arrange flowers.

It is recorded that around 1470, Ikenobo Senkei (also called Sengyo) created a sensation in Kyoto with an arrangement in the Rikka style. This date is often taken as the birth date of formal flower arrangement, although, as we have seen, the *Sendensho* indicates an earlier beginning. While it would be dangerous to assign a definite date to the beginning of flower arranging, we may assume that the first great style of flower arrangement, the Rikka, was formulated during the fifteenth century.

Over the centuries, the influence of China was strong in both the arts and crafts, and this was certainly so during the fifteenth century, as well as the preceding ones. The great Japanese painters of the age worked, for the most part, in the styles of the Sung and Yuan periods (960–1279 and 1280–1368 CE), and Chinese art objects of all sorts—including vases, tables, candleholders, tea vessels, incense burners, and woven silk—were highly prized by the shogun and his entourage as household decorations. The vases and candlesticks shown in early illustrations of five- and three-article flower arrangements have a distinctly Chinese look, and the flower arrangements were designed to accord with these exotic objects.

considered orthodox, although the difficulty of preparing a classic Rikka arrangement is such that most modern arrangers confine themselves to a single vase.

Moving from the Buddhist altars to residences, these upright bouquets of flowers gradually increased in size, and the floral materials acquired an asymmetrical shape. Asymmetry, a fundamental design aspect of Japanese aesthetics, is based on nature and, in particular, on Japanese vistas. Japan is an island country, and its landscape views are generally asymmetric, with mountains on one side and ocean or plain on the other, unlike the scenery of countries on vast continents, such as China.

In Japan, since ancient times, uneven numbers have been used as an aesthetic principle. By 1542, the great flower master Ikenobo Senno had analyzed the Rikka arrangement into seven parts, or "branches," and the style gradually became formalized into the combination of a number of fixed elements. In a general way, the development of the Rikka style resembles that of Oriental ink painting. Over the centuries, so many technical rules were devised that there ceased to be much room for individual expression. On the other hand, the rules were valid to the extent that, by following them, even a person of little artistic ability could produce a work that was visually acceptable, if not inspiring or inspired. While generations of flower arrangers have rebelled against excessive formalization, they have nonetheless accepted the principle of classifying the parts of the arrangement, and at least three of the seven branches of the Rikka form are still regarded as basic.

The fifteenth and sixteenth centuries in Japan were torn by internal warfare, as countless small landowners fought for dominance. After 1550, a succession of great generals gradually unified the country, and a period of general prosperity ensued. The generals and the wealthy of the age constructed castles and palaces whose interiors were decorated with lavish

Sunamono Rikka and its companion Dozuka Rikka. Originally, Sunamono Rikka was created to fit a given space: the decorative shelf next to the *tokonoma* in the complex of Shoin architecture (see page 171). While Rikka is usually upright, Sunamono Rikka is horizontal, because of the space it occupies. On the shelf above the Sunamono Rikka, a miniature Rikka called Dozuka is placed in the center as a complementary arrangement. The arrangements in the photograph shown on page 54 were created as a classic display for the annual exhibition of the Ryusei School; therefore, they are much larger than, for example, the arrangement shown in the drawing at the bottom of page 23. The use of weathered wood creates a dynamic approach to this composition, with colorful flowers kept to a minimum. In the companion Dozuka arrangement, narcissus, japonica, yellow and white chrysanthemums, and branches with colorful leaves are used to create contrasting richness. Note that the *mikoshi* branch of red quince japonica, which is sweeping to the left in the Sunamono, is also found in the Dozuka center, where it sweeps to the right to create unity in the two arrangements.

wall and door paintings, many of them on gold or silver backgrounds. By this time, the shoin zukuri was mature, and the tokonoma decorations–hanging scroll, art object, and flower arrangement–had become the accepted form. The size and décor of the larger houses demanded large and opulent floral arrangements, and the flower arrangers of the time responded with Rikka that were big, colorful, and elaborate.

Sunamono

Sunamono, literally "sand category," is a variation of Rikka. Although it is as rigidly formal as other Rikka arrangements, it has greater boldness and breadth. It is made in a shallow container and is wider than it is high. This style was developed for the grand shoin tokonoma structure. The arrangement was placed on a side shelf, where highly decorated objects, such as an ornate gold lacquer letterbox, were sometimes on display. Sometimes the lower section was used for either a horizontal Rikka arrangement or a display of *chado* ("the way of tea") equipment.

INFORMALITY: ZEN BUDDHISM AND CHADO

Even as the Rikka style was taking form, a very different movement was taking place under the influence of Zen Buddhism and the tea ceremony, which is sometimes referred to today as the "tradition of tea," followed by the name of the school. Both Zen and the ritual drinking of tea were introduced in the late twelfth to early thirteenth centuries, and by the fifteenth century, they had a large following among the upper classes.

Originally, dried tea leaves were boiled and used for medicinal purposes. Eventually the leaves were powdered, which led to the development of chado, the way of tea. Today, both Zen and chado are noted for the strict simplicity of their aesthetic principles, but the tea ceremony was not always as austere as it later became.

In the fifteenth century, it seems to have been less a ritual than an elaborate party, and in the late sixteenth century, a "tea ceremony" was attended by hundreds of guests over a period of ten days. However, practitioners of the tea ceremony favored quiet and refined tastes, and the great sixteenth-century tea master, Sen-no Rikyu, developed a chado that was held in a small rustic hut with a very limited and impeccably simple décor. A noted flower arranger, he sometimes created an arrangement for the tea ceremony that consisted of no more than one flower. Such arrangements were known as Chabana, or "tea flower," and their simplicity represented the complete antithesis of the Rikka style. (See Chabana and Its Relationship to Ikebana on pages 24–25 for a more thorough discussion of Chabana.)

Nageire: The "Thrown-in" Style

Although a special category unto itself, and not in fact a style of Ikebana, Chabana developed from a general class of Ikebana known as Nageire, which comprises all flower arrangements not in the Rikka style. The word Nageire means simply "thrown in," and at first it probably signified not a particular style, but rather the absence of style–that is, merely a spontaneous way

An Edo Period woodblock print showing tea ceremony equipment on display on the decorative shelves adjoining the *tokonoma*. Sunamono Rikka was developed to fit these decorative shelves when tea equipment was not on display.

A woodblock print showing Sunamono Rikka arrangements on display on adjoining decorative shelves. The smaller arrangement on the top shelf is the companion Dozuka, or "miniature Rikka."

CHABANA AND ITS RELATIONSHIP TO IKEBANA

Chabana, a style of flower arranging created for use in the Japanese tea ceremony, is not usually included in a book on Ikebana. However, I often find that Chabana is incorrectly arranged as Ikebana, which is why it is included in this book. Although Japanese "way of tea" chado and tea ceremony gatherings are gaining popularity in the West, information about Chabana is limited. It's important for flower arrangers in the West and new practitioners of chado to understand the purpose of Chabana as well as how it differs from Ikebana.

In a tea ceremony, equipment such as tea bowls, tea caddies, and so on, were originally simple craft art. Throughout history, as generations of tea masters pursued beauty and perfection in the craft of the ceremony, tea equipment evolved to such a level that the crafts involved were elevated to the status of the fine arts–a development that, until recently, was unique in the world of arts. Thus, in a *cha no yu* ("hot water for tea" or "tea ceremony") gathering, the host pays maximum attention to the choice of cast-bronze, cast-iron, ceramic, or bamboo ware, and so on, to complement the season and the purpose for the gathering. It is for this reason that, in Chabana, the flower vase is a revered work of art.

Although the Nageire category of Ikebana has the same technical approach as Chabana, it is very different in concept. A basic rule in a Chabana arrangement is that the flower and other plant materials should be placed in the vase as naturally as pos-sible, without artifice. This means that unusual

Chabana. Vase: Stoneware created by Reiko Koen Kilns. The unique characteristic of Chabana is that in the *tokonoma* of a tearoom, instead of a wall hanging with a Zen statement, often a flower vase with a simple flower arrangement will hang in the center of the wall space. Although it appears to be a simple arrangement, this focal point is visually very important. Upon completion of the arrangement, just before the guests come into the tearoom, it is always important to spray water on the plant to suggest morning dew. The focus of this arrangement is a camellia princess bud.

Chabana. Vase: Handwoven basket. Hypericum blossoms and berries are combined with variegated hosta in a handwoven basket with a handle. So that the visual line of the handle isn't broken, the materials are placed to one side of it. The basket handle should be covered only minimally, and it should never be covered at its center.

Ikebana techniques should be avoided. Flowers that are considered ornate or long lasting, such as chrysanthemums, are generally avoided. Deep red opulent roses or lilies with a strong scent are not used. Simple seasonal but not very common plants are the most appropriate for cha no yu. You should simply hold the materials in your hand—gathering all of the materials in your hand within ten seconds—cut them to the precise length, and then place them in the container immediately. It is thought that if one holds a plant for a longer time, the human ego will wish to change the original natural beauty. Therefore, bending, shaping, and so on is kept to a minimum. Since a tea gathering is based upon the philosophical concept of *ichi-go ichi-e* (literally, "this moment happens once in a lifetime"), nature is being called upon to give the blessing of the season. The arranger's skill is secondary. The vase as an art object takes precedence.

An important distinction between Ikebana (including Nageire) and Chabana is how the arrangements are evaluated. The level of artistry in an Ikebana arrangement is based upon the skill of the creator in using his or her material—how well that arranger can bend, cut, and shape materials for a given pattern. Relative to skill and choice of materials, the flower vase is of less importance.

On the other hand, in Chabana, 60 percent of the artistic value depends on the flower vase, 30 percent on the choice of materials, and only 10 percent on the skill of the arranger.

Chabana. Vase: Basket woven in the style of a fisherman's creel. The flowers, from left to right, are convolvulus, a species of Dietes, and a species of Libertia. Both convolvulus and Dietes have blossoms that last only about a day. The fisherman's creel basket—complete with a cord to tie the creel to a belt—suggests the coolness of water on a warm summer day.

Chabana. Vase: Woven bamboo, from the collection of Mr. Owen Robinson of McLean, Virginia. The Japanese *shobu* iris is arranged in a flower container of fine woven bamboo, in the shape of a hand drum. In Chabana, the iris blossom is brought down close to the rim of the vase, instead of having the long extended stem that is commonly used in Ikebana. However splendid a blossom is, it can be used in this way if it does not overshadow the container.

Below: A *tokonoma* with a Chabana arrangement at the Izumo Cultural Heritage House. A built-in desk appears at the far right of the photograph, underneath the window. (Photo: Tokio Yamanouchi)

Opposite: Seika: Tobi Nejime with sumac and iris. Vase: Contemporary *suiban,* or shallow water tray. This separated arrangement is a variation of Seika. Kabu Wake is a similar variation of Seika and will be found in "The Seika Style," page 88. Both Tobi Nejime and Kabu Wake fall into the category of separated arrangements.

of putting together a floral decoration. The distinctive feature of the Nageire arrangement, from a technical viewpoint, was that the flowers in it were not made to stand erect by artificial means, but were allowed to rest in the vase naturally. Accordingly, the vase used was tall and narrow-mouthed. It was no doubt through the influence of Rikka that Nageire began to acquire certain vague rules; however, probably in reaction to the elaborateness and artificiality of the Rikka style, in Nageire, the natural beauty of flowers was emphasized, and the arranger sought to achieve the effect of flowers growing wild in a wood or field.

It is by no means accidental that the Rikka style is associated with the more traditional forms of Buddhism, while the Nageire style is associated with Zen, for Rikka arrangements grew from a philosophic attempt to conceive an organized universe, while Nageire arrangements represent an attempt to achieve immediate oneness with the universe. The Rikka arrangement is an appropriate offering to be placed before the Buddha, but a Nageire arrangement is a direct link between human beings and their natural surroundings. One style is conceptual and idealistic, the other instinctive and naturalistic. The difference is similar to that between the arduous philosophic study associated with traditional Buddhism and the direct enlightenment of Zen Buddhism.

The Nageire style was especially popular during the seventeenth century, which was also the golden age of Rikka. The fact that these two contrasting styles came into their own almost simultaneously is not surprising, when one considers that this was the age when the rich lived in large and lavish houses, yet retreated for spiritual comfort to diminutive and bucolic teahouses.

Commoners and the merchant classes also welcomed Nageire as a freer way to appreciate the beauty of nature, since unlike Rikka, it was not hampered with a set of rules. From a very practical point of view, the Nageire style was

bound to gain wider appeal than the Rikka because it could be put together from a limited number of materials in a short time, whereas Rikka required many materials, highly developed techniques, a good deal of time, and much more space for display. Generally speaking, Rikka was appropriate in large houses or monastic reception halls, but Nageire could be a thing of beauty in the smallest and most humble dwelling.

SEIKA: SIMPLICITY AND FORMALITY

Once professional flower arrangers had established the composition and structure for Rikka, exhibitions led to competition, which in turn spurred on the quest for novelty for its own sake. Branches were cut into pieces and reassembled to form extreme twisted lines; even the legs of a living hawk were tied down to a branch as part of the arrangement. Such extreme practices, done just for the sake of competition, startled the visiting public and led to the loss of Rikka's natural beauty. On record are comments that Rikka had became a fossilized art. At the same time, the new form of cultural activity, chado, was competing with Rikka for the patronage of the court nobility and warrior classes. Thus, Rikka entered a long period of stagnation.

By the seventeenth century, the court nobility were no longer dominant, and Japanese architectural styles adjusted to the needs of the warrior classes. A third group, the commoners or merchant classes, also influenced cultural changes with their education, tastes, and financial power, which often surpassed that of the warrior classes. A less formal version of the shoin evolved known as the *sukiya.* It displayed a simple elegance. This movement influenced Japanese architectural styles and eventually became what is now called the traditional Japanese house. The major feature in these homes was the tokonoma, the special space for the arts. Toward the beginning of the eighteenth century, this gave rise to a new type of flower arrangement called Seika, which literally means "fresh-living flowers." The formal display in the tokonoma was established as a trio: a wall hanging, flower arrangement, and incense burner.

The Seika style is also known by the name Shoka. The words seika and *shoka* are variant readings of the same two written ideograms. The first ideogram can be read as *sei, sho,* or *ike,* which means "fresh." The second ideogram can be read as *ka, hana,* or *bana* and means "flowers." In general, present-day members of the Ikenobo School use the term Shoka, but members of other schools prefer Seika. The same word can also be used to refer to Ikebana, but this reading did not become a part of the vernacular until the nineteenth century.

After nearly a century of mutual influence between the two styles of Rikka and Nageire, Seika emerged, retaining some of the principles of Rikka, but in a much simplified form. In the Seika style, living materials of branches, grasses, and flowers were arranged to create line, plane, and mass in a given space, with divisions that included "active empty space"– which was equal in importance to the natural plant materials. In a Seika arrangement, which is placed in a tokonoma, the "active empty space" both within the arrangement and within the frame of the tokonoma are vitally important.

Above: **Niju Ike Seika in Tomo Taisaki style.** Vase: Bamboo tube.
This dynamic arrangement of white gentian is in the informal Seika style.
As Seika matured, it began to develop many variations in style. Generally,
taisaki arrangements are of differing materials, but *tomo taisaki* means
that in this arrangement all three elements are of the same plant materials.

Opposite: **Seika in a traditional manner.** Vase: Bronze with motif of
Chinese relief. The materials are cherry blossoms with pine.

The concept of active empty space is found in painting composition and dry landscape Zen gardens and parallels the
"active silence" in the music of Noh theater. Active silence, or in
Haiku poetry "active suggestion"–the absence or silence that
cannot be expressed by words–forms an important and unique
feature in all of the Japanese fine arts. In contrast, traditional
Western arts, enrich the given space or time to its fullest.

In the Seika style, three of the original seven branches of
the Rikka arrangement, *shin, soe,* and *uke* were retained,
although uke came to be known as *taisaki*–literally, the tip
of *tai.*) Shin, which was the central branch, was the tallest;
soe, which branched off to one side, came next; and taisaki
branched off in the other direction, creating an uneven or
scalene triangle. Much of the simplicity of the Nageire style
was retained, and only a limited variety of plants were used.
The typical Seika arrangement was much smaller than Rikka,
and so it was suitable for use in an ordinary tokonoma. At the
same time, the Seika style was more formal than Nageire, not
only because the general position of the three principal
branches was fixed, but because the arrangement was made
to appear to rise from a single stalk. Whether the vase was
tall and narrow-mouthed or low and wide-mouthed, the stems
of the various parts were held together near the base with
a wooden or metal device, so that the whole arrangement
rose straight up from the center of the container. In addition,
each individual branch is skillfully placed from behind, one
after another. It is for this reason that the viewer who
attempts to see the arrangement from the side is considered
disrespectful.

The possibilities for variation were great, and many different types of Seika developed, becoming the focal points of a
number of schools. The arrangements shown on this page
and the next illustrate two of the many possible variations of
Seika. In 1766 there appeared a book called *Seika Hyoban
Tosei Kakinozoki (A Look at Today's Popular Seika Styles),*
which gives an indication of the proliferation of schools:

> Popular schools of this age include the Old Senke
> School, the Enshu School, the Yoken School, the Irie
> School, the Tanno-sen School, the Genji School, the
> Shofu School, the Senkega School and the "Only" Old
> School. The Ikenobo family heads the original school of
> Rikka, but there is also a split from this form known as
> the Seika.

In addition to the various schools named in the *Seika
Hyoban Tosei Kakinozoki,* there were minor subdivisions
within each school, many of which in turn became entirely
separate. One of these was the Ryusei School, which origi-
nated within the Ikenobo School but separated from it in
1884. The Ryusei School, whose tenets form the basis for the
lessons in this book, and whose members prepared the
arrangements reproduced here, has one distinctive feature in
common with the parent Ikenobo School: it still maintains
the ancient art of the Rikka style, which has always
demanded the highest degree of technical skill. Yet the
Ryusei School continues to develop simplified techniques
with a more natural use of materials. Within the school, some
of the largest arrangements are patterned after the original
Rikka and are called Ubu Rikka (*ubu* means "fresh"). Other
schools have for the most part dropped Rikka because of the
time and effort the style demands.

During the Edo period (1615–1868), Japan was almost entirely cut off from the rest of the world. The Tokugawa shogunate, which governed the country during this era, forbade all exchanges between Japan and other nations, except for a small amount of commerce with the Dutch and Chinese through the port of Nagasaki for trade and medicine. While the purpose of this policy of seclusion was ostensibly to protect the nation against foreign invasion, infiltration, or exploitation, the shogunate's principal aim seems to have been to stabilize its own rule by preventing changes that might result from foreign influences. During this time a stable social structure remained intact, and there was little or no internal warfare. All things considered, the Tokugawa succeeded to a remarkable extent, for they managed to stay in power for two and a half centuries, with any social adjustments taking place beneath the seemingly unruffled surface.

No one can stop time, of course, and little by little Japan was changing from a rice economy to a money economy. Dutch medicine, called *rangaku*, and other forms of European culture gradually filtered in, influencing Japanese culture and the arts. In the arts, a seclusion policy has a tendency to cause stagnation. In painting, Western influences such as linear perspective did seep in, influencing a group of artists who began to incorporate the new techniques into their works. A significant development in the arts during the Edo period was the woodblock print, which continued to flourish, but in painting and architecture there was a pronounced trend toward formalism and academicism. Broadly speaking, there was more and more attention to technical detail, and less and less creative inspiration.

By the latter part of the eighteenth century, the orthodox and largest school of painting—called the Kano School—had grown so arid that a number of independently minded painter-scholars rebelled against it and developed very free and personal styles of their own. Their works came to be known as *bunjin-ga* (paintings by men of letters). During the late eighteenth and early nineteenth centuries, men from the same group of literati created a similar movement in the field of flower arrangement, developing a number of free styles known collectively as *bunjin-ike* (arrangements by men of letters). The bunjin-ike, like the bunjin-ga, was a revolt against orthodoxy.

The West has often marveled at the speed with which Japan adopted Occidental ways after the opening of the country in the second half of the nineteenth century. Not only the political system, but the economy and the social organization changed in a matter of two or three decades, and this change was amply reflected in the arts, which almost immediately began to show the influence of nineteenth-century Europe. The rapidity of Japan's transformation was largely owing to the fact that the system so long maintained by the shogunate had lost a great deal of its vitality and meaning. Technically, the Tokugawa government was overthrown by a coalition of clans favoring the restoration of power to the emperor, but more likely, the shogunate collapsed of its own dead weight and weakness. In the same fashion, Japanese art appeared to virtually collapse before the onslaught of Western culture, but this was because the new was an exciting form of change.

It would be difficult to prove that flower arrangement became as formalistic and superficial as, say, painting in this period, for the actual arrangements no longer exist. The proliferation of schools emphasizing one or another variation on the Seika style suggests to the student of Japanese art history that flower arrangers were dividing up and taking sides over relatively minor points, rather than developing new ideas.

It is an important reminder that a thread of stability was retained in the traditional arts of Japan because of the long-established custom of the *iemoto* system, whereby the eldest son or some designated person took over the reins of authority as head of a school. This designated grandmaster was given the task of charting the school's direction, of preserving the unique and valuable aspects in the art of that school, even while new creativity developed. This practice continues today for all the traditional arts—theater, music, dance, painting, flower arranging, chado, and others.

MODERN IKEBANA: MORIBANA TO FREESTYLE

The introduction of Western culture to Japan was bound to affect flower arranging, if only because of the appearance of new flowers from abroad and the architectural influence of the Western-style rooms that were being built. The traditional way of arranging flowers was more resistant to change than traditional painting or architecture because an organized Western system for arranging flowers did not exist. Ikebana at its most prosaic was a more highly developed art than anything similar in the West. This was recognized early on, so in this case the principal influence was that of Japan on the Occident. In one respect, the Westernization of Japan strengthened traditional Ikebana, for after 1888 flower arrangement was adopted as a part of the standard curriculum for girls in the Western-inspired public education system.

Nevertheless, the impact of the Occident began to show up in floral arrangements. By 1907 the flower master Unshin Ohara was exhibiting Ikebana in which he used flowers of Western origin. Ohara was a member of the Ikenobo School at the time, but he subsequently broke away and set up a new school, the Ohara School, which is still one of the largest and most prominent schools in Japan. Ohara created the style that featured shallow containers and free placement of branches, which came to be known as Moribana, literally "a mass of flowers." Much freer in approach than the Seika style, Moribana rapidly became the most popular style of all.

Originally, a box with movable partitions was devised, which could be adjusted to the thickness of the stems of flowers and branches, to keep the plant materials upright. The major innovation in the late nineteenth century was the *kenzan*, a flat, heavy metal holder with vertical needles on which branches and stems can be impaled. The kenzan is used in somewhat the same fashion as the frog (a common glass or metal piece with holes in it), but it permits freer placement and positioning of flowers, since the stems can be firmly affixed to it at almost any angle. The kenzan is also more easily concealed than the usual frog. In a sense, the kenzan is the technical base without which the Moribana style could not exist, for without it, free and varied arrangements of plants in shallow containers would be almost impossible. Although many translations of the word kenzan are possible, the most typical gives *ken* as "sword" and *an* or *san* as "mountain." However, none of the translations is entirely satisfactory, and in this book the Japanese word is retained.

In the Showa (1926–1989) and Heisei (1990 to the present) periods, the Moribana style has given rise to still freer and more imaginative free-creative forms, such as Jiyu-ka (meaning "free flowers") and Zen'ei-ka (meaning "avant-garde flowers"). In this book the latter is called the abstract style. Jiyu-ka are created with floral materials. The Zen'ei-ka style incorporates metals and other man-made materials.

Other than being required to include one natural material–living or dried–in their arrangements, abstract arrangers are comparatively unbound by rules. In addition to all kinds of living plants and flowers, they make use of dried materials–left natural, bleached, or painted–and pieces of metal, glass, stone, concrete, and the like.

Many abstract arrangements contain no flowers at all and could, but for the fact that they are created by flower arrangers, more properly be classified as abstract sculpture (for examples, see pages 32 and 130–31). This has led some people to complain that Ikebana is being killed by iconoclastic modernists, but a more judicious view is that the art of flower arranging is growing and expanding to satisfy the requirements and creative urges of our time. But the fact remains that the wildest of the abstractionists are grounded in the fundamental techniques of the ancient tradition, and many of them perform the vital task of transmitting these principles to large numbers of followers. Moreover, the abstract designers are as much concerned with the fundamental problem of producing an aesthetically satisfying design as are the sternest traditionalists.

In Japan today, millions of people continue to study Ikebana, delighting both themselves and others with their creative work. In large cities there are constant exhibitions by one or another of the many schools of Ikebana, and publications devoted entirely to floral art are legion. No other art displays such vitality on both the professional, amateur and popular levels. This vitality has been rapidly transmitted to other countries through organizations such as Ikebana International.

Ikebana as it is being creatively developed today has inspired and influenced a new genre in the world of art called "installation art" (see page 33). Many artists, especially sculp-

Moribana Style: Formal Basic Pattern. Vase: Ryusei School ceramic *suiban*. In Moribana, the three major branches of Seika—*shin*, *soe*, and *taisaki*—are used; the difference is the use of the contemporary *kenzan*. The accompanying flowers are simple in appearance, yet the arrangement is graceful. A beginning student in Ikebana will start with learning how to make this arrangement, as a foundation in this art. The materials are pussy willow branches, with catkins, and yellow chrysanthemums.

tors, have received recognition throughout the world with their temporary installation art.

Contemporary Japanese architecture is dramatically changing, and the choice of floral arranging materials, and the manner of displaying them, will continue to change with it. The following arrangements show the direction that Ikebana is moving toward in the twenty-first century, but these creations are all by artists who have been thoroughly trained in classical Ikebana.

Left: **Contemporary Freestyle: Tai Saku.** Vase: Contemporary ceramic. Pine branches with thick limbs form this dynamic and large composition (*tai* means "*large*" and *saku* "arrangement"). A large contemporary vase is used for this arrangement, and the artist had to pay close attention to the total balance to make the work stand freely and securely. The overall effect of this arrangement is the feeling of a work in contemporary calligraphy. Along with pine branches of variegated pine needles, the other plant materials are bittersweet vines with red berries, yellow button mums, and white camellia with leaves. The arrangement measures about six feet in height and six feet in width.

Right: **Contemporary installation art Ikebana.** Contemporary Ikebana has taken the innovative route by moving from the indoors to the outdoors. Arrangements are no longer limited to a *tokonoma* or a living room. In this work, poppies of various colors are attached to the entrance to a building.

Left: **Freestyle arrangement.** Vase: Glass *suiban*. The focus for the Ryusei School's studies in contemporary Ikebana goes beyond using flowers for arrangements, thus giving rise to unique creativity. Large leaves of paulonia have been made soft and pliable and wrapped around white eggplants, which have then been stacked up inside a glass vase. This imaginative use of materials makes this a wonderful unit. A stem of the paulonia forms a straight line on the left to give a distinctive accent to the total creation.

PART II

Styles of Ikebana

The Rikka Style

The Rikka style of today has developed into an elaborate form of arrangement, yet the materials form a tight group as they rise from the middle of the vase opening. The visual image suggests a ballerina dancing on her toes, with her graceful movement and pose crystallized. Rikka is a refined and elegant form, which we call the "Queen of Ikebana." Queen Rikka is meant to be admired as an art form by the viewer.

Rikka was highly supported by the court nobility, the cultural salon of the past. However, in later years (from the seventeenth to eighteenth centuries), commoners began to take part in creating Rikka, leading to the creation of other styles. Eventually the various lines and empty spaces in Rikka arrangements were given names and positions. The key branches and their positions are called *yaku eda* (*yaku* meaning "position," *eda* meaning "branch").

Rikka, along with the Seika style, comprises a classic category in Ikebana in which the inherited traditional form must be totally understood before the Ikebana artist begins to exercise individual creativity within the framework.

Ikebana, though a classic art, is not fixed. Rather, in each generation, masters have been able to polish and perfect the art–just as, in music, the same composition is performed and interpreted by different generations of musicians. The talent and sensitivity of the composer, conductor, and performers influence the outcome for the audience.

Rikka's structural rules–called positions–guide the basic composition of the style. It is essential that these positions be honored. Doing so, with the understanding that within this structure there is room for personal expression, is the secret to Rikka.

THE NINE KEY RIKKA POSITIONS

The nine key positions in a Rikka arrangement were developed by the Buddhist monks, who incorporated Buddhist teachings into their flower arrangements. The terms they developed are still in use today.

The two diagrams on page 38 show the order and placement of plant materials in Rikka arrangements. To create Rikka, the following nine key positions must be filled, to form a skeletal structure.

Left: **A rendering of a woodblock print from the Early Edo period (1615–1868). The print shows a samurai and his family admiring a Rikka arrangement created for the New Year's celebration.**

Opposite: **Rikka: Noki Shin in right-hand pattern.** Vase: Contemporary white glaze. In this arrangement, summer sumac with its branch of naturally contrasting thicknesses is carefully and cleverly utilized for dynamic effect. *Shin* and *uke* are formed from summer sumac. Spindle tree forms *soe* and *nagashi*. *Sho shin* is formed of dark purple *kakitsubata* iris bud. *Mae oki* is variegated hosta; *do* is Japanese yew; *hikae* is the orange lily bud; underneath *hikae* is *kusa dome* of fringed pink. Underneath *nagashi* is *ki dome* of cypress leaves; *aizashi* is balloon flower. This combination of materials gives the refreshing feeling of the cool breezes of summer.

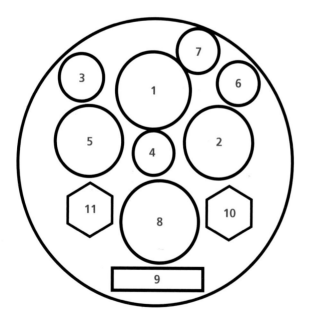

Below: This diagram shows the angle of placement for the eleven units. The basic nine positions—the *yaku eda*—form the outline of the entire arrangement. The two additional positions of *ki dome* and *kusa dome* are used as the final touch—or, in other words, as a "visual period." Some arrangements may not need these two additional elements, but line materials with an absence of leaves and flowers may need both the *ki dome* and *kusa dome*.

Bottom: **This diagram shows the location of the eleven positions in the vase.**

Opposite: **These nine diagrams illustrate the most commonly used variations in Rikka. The more serous reader can use these diagrams to study how the Rikka arrangements on pages 42–57 were created.**

1. **Shin** ("main high point," also known as "spiritual mountain")
2. **Uke** ("summit one can reach," also known as "receiving")
3. **Hikae** ("achieving balance," also known as "reserve" or "waiting")
4. **Sho shin** ("central point," also known as "waterfall"
5. **Soe** ("secondary or supporting branch")
6. **Nagashi** ("stream")
7. **Mikoshi** ("mist dividing the sacred from the common," also known as "overlook")
8. **Do** ("body"; *Note:* Many different plant materials may be required to conceal the technical component.)
9. **Mae oki** ("front body," or additional body)

The following are two accompanying positions to the nine main positions:

10. **Ki dome** ("village," or final conclusion using branch or tree materials. Also known as "branches and berries from the countryside")
11. **Kusa dome** ("city," also known as "final conclusion"; *Note:* Often colorful flowers are used.)

Ikebana is a visual art that uses plant materials that come in a wide variety of forms. Depending upon the materials, artistic judgment must be used to readjust the established formulas. These readjustments reveal the skill of the arranger. The following positions—a through e—are placed next to the position they support and are used whenever the arranger thinks they are necessary. Some floral materials have abundant leaves or flowers and thus may not require these additions. Some floral materials, however, may require additions to fill the open spaces. (A beginner will not need to know these terms, but an experienced Ikebana artist should know these terms and their uses.)

a. **Do uchi** ("inner do")
b. **Do gakoi** ("frame of do")
c. **Iro kiri** ("color separation")
d. **Ura gakoi** ("back covering")
e. **Aizashi** ("open space that must be filled in with proper color and texture")

Variations in Rikka

Many different Rikka variations have been developed throughout the centuries. The diagrams opposite are the nine basic variations in pattern, and a few others in addition to these. Two basic styles are Sugu Shin and Noki Shin.

Sugu Shin refers to a form that rises straight from the base to the top of the arrangement (*sugu* means "straight," and *shin* means "main branch"). Noki Shin refers to a shin that begins at the bottom center, then curves left or right, and then, at its top, is straight above the base. A third variant, called Fukyu no Shin, has recently been developed. Its shin begins from the bottom center, but the tip does not reach the centerline, which is called *chu shin*. This gives the top part of the arrangement an open feeling.

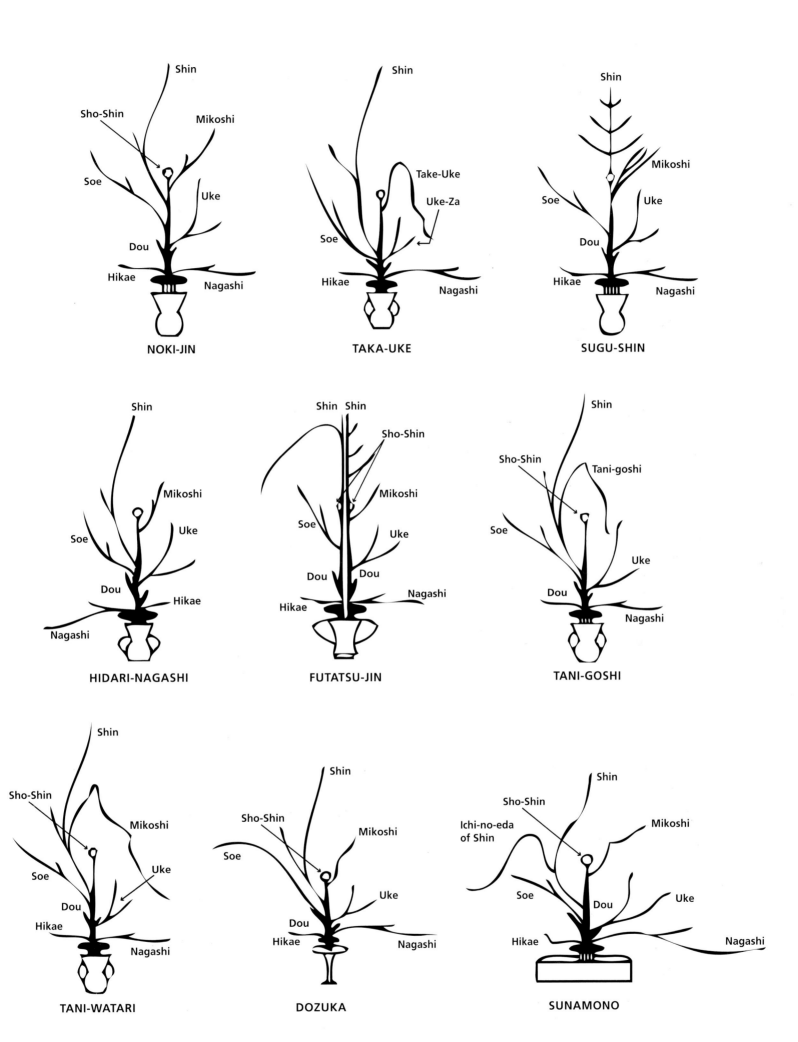

NOKI-JIN

Shin
Sho-Shin
Mikoshi
Soe
Uke
Dou
Hikae
Nagashi

TAKA-UKE

Shin
Take-Uke
Uke-Za
Soe
Hikae
Nagashi

SUGU-SHIN

Shin
Mikoshi
Soe
Uke
Dou
Hikae
Nagashi

HIDARI-NAGASHI

Shin
Mikoshi
Soe
Uke
Dou
Hikae
Nagashi

FUTATSU-JIN

Shin   Shin
Sho-Shin
Mikoshi
Soe
Uke
Dou   Dou
Hikae
Nagashi

TANI-GOSHI

Shin
Sho-Shin
Tani-goshi
Soe
Uke
Dou
Nagashi

TANI-WATARI

Shin
Sho-Shin
Mikoshi
Soe
Uke
Dou
Hikae
Nagashi

DOZUKA

Shin
Sho-Shin
Mikoshi
Soe
Uke
Dou
Hikae
Nagashi

SUNAMONO

Shin
Sho-Shin
Ichi-no-eda of Shin
Mikoshi
Soe
Uke
Dou
Hikae
Nagashi

Below: **A classic Rikka arrangement in the Sugu Shin category.**

Opposite, bottom: **A classic three-vase Rikka arrangement created for the audience hall in Edo Castle. It is attributed to Ikenobo Senmyo XLI, who was active in the early nineteenth century. (Drawing by the author, 1963).** Today it is almost impossible to see a large three-vase Rikka arrangement. The reader can only surmise how grand these arrangements could have been from these drawings. Symbolically, Buddha is in the center, with the Sun Bodhisattva to his right and the Moon Bodhisattva to his left.

VASES FOR RIKKA

In Rikka, customarily a heavy flower vase of cast bronze is used. Some contemporary forms give a very light feeling, but in actuality, they are all very heavy. Since the arrangements are generally large, and many different materials are used, the physical balance (left to right and back to front) is different from the artistic visual balance. If the creator of Rikka does not consider the physical balance, the arrangement will often fall over. For this reason, heavy cast-bronze vases are a favorite for Rikka artists. If the vase is light, the bottom is filled with pebbles or other heavier materials to weigh it down. You will see a variety of Rikka vases—traditional cast bronze and contemporary ceramic—in the following arrangements.

Left-Hand and Right-Hand Patterns

The diagrams on the previous page are samples of a left-hand pattern. The traditional terminology for left-hand patterns in Ikebana is *hon-gatte* (*hon* means "main"; *gatte* means "side"). *Gyaku-gatte* (*gyaku* mean "reverse") is the right-hand pattern. This concept is based upon the religious altars where the Buddha was placed in the center, with the Sun Bodhisattva on his right and the Moon Bodhisattva to his left. From paintings to Ikebana, this convention is used.

If the arrangement (see the drawing at the bottom of page 41) is considered to take place with the Buddha facing the viewer, then the arrangement on the viewer's left is on the Buddha's right, thus creating the somewhat confusing tradition of calling an arrangement whose main branch curves to the left, a "right-hand" arrangement, and one whose main emphasis seems to be on the right, a "left-hand" arrangement. (The right hand is always the important one in the Far East because the right hand is considered the standard form, especially in calligraphy.)

CLASSIC RIKKA

In the early sixties, while preparing the Ikebana examples for the original edition of *The Art of Arranging Flowers*, I relied upon many "elder masters" to create the classic Rikka arrangement in the Sugu Shin style shown to the right. The accepted technique in those days was to follow very classic traditions. The twisted pine branches on the right-hand side were reassembled from small pieces, to give a unique effect. Pine branches about a foot long were cut, and the limbs and pine needles removed for reassembling. Each pine needle grouping was reassembled in an idealized formation, then wired to the limbs, which were then rewired to the foot-long bare branches in an almost fish-bone pattern. These sets of pine-branch units were slid onto nails that protruded from the main trunk (see page 154). The assembly of these short branches of pine needles, in the required forms and lengths, takes four masters a full day to complete. Every chrysanthemum blossom had a copper wire attached underneath the stem with thin wire, and every leaf was reinforced with a thin wire so it could be bent into the proper position. It required another full day of labor-intensive treatment to prepare the chrysanthemum blossoms so that they could be adjusted to the desired angle and direction and remain that way. A total of three days, with four people working intensively, was required to complete the project. Since pine needles arranged in this fashion have no way of obtaining water, they must constantly be sprayed with sake, whose sugar coats the needles while the alcohol evaporates. This helps to hold the original moisture in the needle. This gorgeous Rikka arrangement is a labor-intensive project that will last for a maximum of five days in good condition.

The three woodblock prints of Rikka arrangements at the top of the opposite page are from a popular publication of the Edo period (1615–1868) for Ikebana enthusiasts. The artist was Ikenobo Semyo, the forty-first generation of grandmasters of the Ikenobo School, from which the Ryusei School evolved.

Below, left: This arrangement is made in the *Kusa Isshiki* style, which uses only flower materials. Iris and lotus are used for this arrangement, which was created in 1862.

Below, middle: This unique Rikka is an evocation of the phoenix, symbolic in the Far East for longevity and nobility. This arrangement was created for the New Year's celebration in 1822. The weeping willow serves as shin for wings, and weathered wood is cleverly used as the neck and head of the bird. Other plant materials form the tail feathers.

Below, right: This arrangement is a gorgeous double *shin* style Rikka. Double *shin* arrangements are considered the ultimate splendor in Rikka. Two entirely different sets of materials are used for the two sides, yet they balance to make one whole. A hand held straight on its edge can be passed from top to bottom between the two sides.

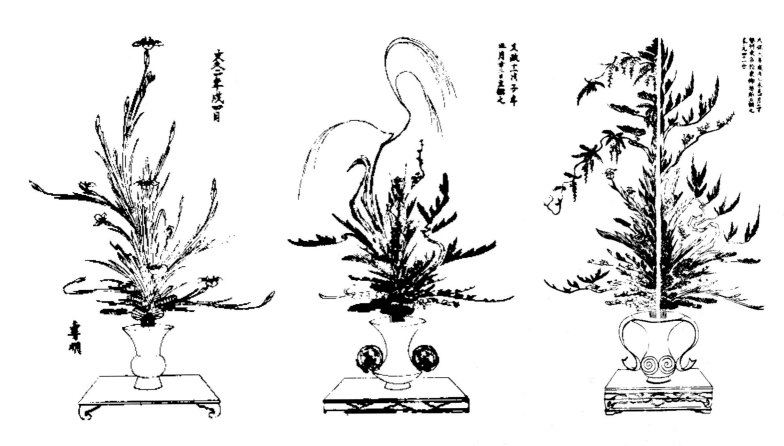

Above: **Rikka: Noki Shin in right-hand pattern with pine branches.** Vase: Cast bronze in the style of an ancient Chinese wine goblet. In this arrangement, created for the New Year celebration, young pine branches are used for the three important positions of *shin*, *uke*, and *hikae*. The fluid lines of quince japonica make up *soe* and *nagashi*, and the sweeping curve of the weeping willow forms *mikoshi*. The narcissus flowers and leaf blades form *sho shin*. The mass of small leaves of the azalea branch form *do*. *Mae oki* is formed from Japanese yew. Camellia forms *ki dome* at the right; small white chrysanthemums form *kusa dome*; red berries form *aizashi*.

Opposite: **Ubu Rikka: Sugu Shin Rikka.** Vase: Contemporary ceramic with a blue glaze. This is in the Hidari Nagashi style, thus *nagashi* is on the left-hand side, and *hikae* is on the right. Compared to classic Rikka (see page 40), with its reassembled pine branches—grand in appearance but static in feel—Sugu Shin Rikka is refreshingly fluid. *Ubu* means "fresh" or "as they are." Therefore, rather than any artificiality in joining plant materials, the natural shapes of the plants are used in this style. The stately white *shobu* (Japanese iris) grows straight up from muddy water with its erect swordlike leaves. The Japanese iris is symbolic for manliness and is traditionally the flower for Boys' Day on May 5. On the right-hand side, the gentle curves of spirea form the attendant branch of *soe*. Forsythia branches form *mikoshi*, *uke*, and *nagashi*. Lily buds form *hikae*, and yellow chrysanthemums take on the position of *sho shin*.

Above: **Rikka: Noki Shin in right-hand pattern.** Vase: Contemporary cast bronze. The sweeping lines of the weeping willow branch, which forms *shin*, give this Rikka arrangement a unique charm. The thin lines spread out to create a large active space. Underneath the willow, *soe* and *nagashi* are camellia branches. *Uke* and *hikae* are *senryo*, or Chloranthus glaber, with red berries and green leaves. Flowers are usually used for *sho shin*, but in this case a straight young pine is utilized and combined with narcissus to create a nice central stability. To the left of *sho shin*, fasciated willow is *mikoshi*; *do* is a yew species, with yellow chrysanthemums, called *do uchi*, used as an accent. The small white chrysanthemums form *mae oki* and *kusa dome*; at the left, red azalea flowers and a branch are *ki dome*. Since this arrangement is focused on the *shin* with the weeping willow, other than *sho shin*, the key position branches reflect spaciousness.

Opposite: **Rikka: Noki Shin in right-hand pattern.** Vase: Contemporary cast bronze. In this arrangement, the Japanese flowering apricot is used for *shin* and *uke*. *Soe* is a sweeping azalea branch that veers to the right. *Nagashi*, extending to the left, is also an azalea branch. *Sho shin* is the white chrysanthemum, and *mikoshi* is the raspberry branch, immediately to the left and above *sho shin*. Hikae is camellia; *mae oki* is boxwood; *kusa dome*, at bottom left, is small white chrysanthemums; and *ki dome*, at bottom right, is raspberry. In the space between key placements, called *aizashi* (*ai* means "between"), cypress leaves and variegated hydrangea branch are used.

Rikka: Noki Shin in right-hand pattern. Vase: Contemporary cast bronze. In this arrangement, *shin* is formed from white quince japonica. Its dynamic movement contrasts with the highly angled *nagashi* (called *chu dan nagashi*). Tight buds of white magnolia form *uke* and *hikae*. *Soe* and *ki dome* are formed from the red camellia. *Sho shin* is iris; *mikoshi* is spirea, and *do* is variegated Japanese cypress leaves. *Mae oki* is boxwood; *kusa dome* is formed with small purple chrysanthemums. Yellow chrysanthemums are used as an accent for *do uchi*. This composition conveys a powerful sense of extravagant liveliness.

Rikka: Noki Shin in left-hand pattern. Vase: Contemporary blue-glazed ceramic. Summer sumac is used for *shin* and *uke* in this Rikka arrangement. *Soe* and *nagashi* are pink azaleas. *Mikoshi* is spirea; *sho shin* is white peony; *do* is Japanese cypress leaves; *mae oki* is variegated Japanese euonymus; *hikae* is orange lily with its bud, and underneath it, white chrysanthemums are *kusa dome*. The camellia leaves and branch are *ki dome*. Yellow chrysanthemums and small white chrysanthemums are the *do uchi*. *Aizashi* are purple bachelor's buttons between *sho shin* and *uke*. The overall feeling of openness and of an early summer day is enhanced by the pink azaleas.

Above: **Rikka: Noki Shin in left-hand pattern.** Vase: Contemporary cast bronze. This arrangement, utilizing autumnal materials for the main focus, provides a refreshing change. The seven autumnal plants are traditional for autumn festivities in Japan. In this arrangement, yellow patrinia, one of the most favored of the seven autumnal plants, forms the *shin* and *uke*. While it is a slender forb, it grows straight and tall, so eulalia, or *Miscanthus*, grass is used in association with it, to provide graceful and curving lines. *Soe* is a spirea branch; *sho shin* is purple gentian. *Do* is Japanese yew, and white chrysanthemums accent it as *do uchi*. Nagashi is fasciated willow, and underneath are small white chrysanthemums, which are used as *ki dome* and echo the *do uchi*. On the opposite side, the coxcomb is *hikae*. Underneath *hikae* is a pink gentian as *kusa dome*. *Mae oki* is coltsfoot leaves.

Opposite: Rikka: right-hand pattern of Taka Uke (*taka* means "high"). Vase: Contemporary white-glazed ceramic. *Shin* and *uke* are pine in this arrangement, the use of which is a very unusual feature, especially in the line of *uke*. *Uke* usually lies at a lower position and rises up at the left. In this arrangement, the bold, thick pine branch rises up and then sweeps down, creating a movement that is both strong and dramatic. *Soe* is quince japonica, and underneath it is also a varie-gated pine-needle branch as *hikae*. As the "Queen of Ikebana," the ballerina on her toes, Rikka requires a tremendous sense of balance. Although there is dynamic movement in the composition, the three positions of the pine branches create a great sense of stability. The deep pink quince japonica as *soe* on the right is similar in line quality and mirrors the color of the leaves of sumac forming the *nagashi*, which also gives nice balance. *Sho shin* is the white chrysanthemums. While *mikoshi* has been eliminated, the peak of the curvature of the *taka uke* branch takes the place of *mikoshi* as well. Spirea in autumnal colors functions as *uchi zoe*—which is often found in the classic form of Rikka known as Sunamono (see page 23). The *uchi zoe* position fills the space between the *sho shin* and the extended curvature of the *shin* trunk. *Do* and *mae oki* are formed from variegated euonymus. To the right of the euonymus are small red chrysanthemums (as *kusa dome*); on the opposite side are white camellias (as *ki dome*). To fill up the space between *taka uke*, *soe*, and *nagashi*, three purple gentians form *aizashi*. On the opposite side, the one white medium-sized chrysanthemum is also *aizashi*.

Above: **Rikka: Dozuka (also spelled Doudzuka) category.** Vase: Traditional cast bronze. Compared to the standard size of Rikka, a *dozuka* arrangement is, in a sense, a miniaturized Rikka. For this reason, the entire concept of arrangement is for it to be an accompaniment to the grand Sunamono in the *tokonoma* beneath it, and the materials chosen are therefore light and petite. (See page 23 for a discussion of the development of the Sunamono category of Rikka.) *Shin* and *nagashi* are azalea branches; *uke* and *hikae* are pine branches; *soe* and *mikoshi* are dark pink quince; and *sho shin* is an iris in full bloom, accompanied by tight buds. *Do* is formed from a species of juniper, accented by *do uchi* of yellow chrysanthemums. *Mae oki* is small white chrysanthemums; *kusa dome* is the light-colored "fringed pink"; and *ki dome* is quince. Originally, *dozuka* arrangements were straight, but recently many variations have been developed.

Opposite: **Rikka: Fukyu no Shin.** Vase: Contemporary ceramic. Traditionally in classic Ikebana styles, such as Rikka and Seika, *shin* (the main position) always rises straight from the center of the flower vase, and the top of *shin* returns back to the center of the arrangement, thus giving it a very formal or regal aura. However, when one sees trees or plants in nature, often they do not necessarily grow directly above their roots. Based upon these observations, the Ryusei School has developed additional categories in recent years. These categories can be translated as *fukyu* or "not reached." This means that the top of *shin* does not return to the center. With this concept in mind, the area above the flower vase opens up to the left or right of the center, and a more relaxed and natural-istic atmosphere is created. The following three examples are in this Fukyu category. Many variations in eulalia, or *Miscanthus*, grass can be found. Making use of the graceful curvatures of this variegated *Miscanthus* grass, *shin* and *uke* create an open and benevolent aura. *Uke* usually branches out with the end facing up, but in this case, the law of nature is utilized in an artistic manner. *Soe* and *nagashi* are mountain ash with berries. *Hikae* is the red-orange lily buds. *Sho shin* is *kakitsubata* iris blossom with two accompanying buds. *Mikoshi*, to the right of *sho shin*, is a spirea branch. *Do* and *mae oki* are boxwood, and *do uchi* is formed of yellow chrysanthemums. Underneath *do* and *mae oki* are white chrysanthemums as *iro kiri* ("color separation"). *Kusa dome* and *aizashi* are purple balloon flowers (Chinese bell flowers). Due to the leaves and flowers of *nagashi*, *ki dome* is not necessary and has been eliminated.

Rikka: Fukyu no Shin. The stargazer lily is one of the most opulent members of the family of lilies. This hybrid version is a modern development, and therefore is suitable for contemporary Rikka. In this Fukyu no Shin arrangement, with the *shin* slightly off center to the left, the sense of the weight of this gorgeous flower is enhanced. For balance, *uke* is also of the same flower. The characteristic sweeping lines of Korean forsythia branches, used for the *soe* and *nagashi* positions, contrast with the stargazers' straight stems, beautifully capturing a sense of rhythm and movement. Another type of variegated *Miscanthus zebrinus* (hawk's feathers, or zebra grass) is used for *mikoshi*. The opened orange lily blossom is *hikae*; pink flowers and leaves of "tigers tail" form *sho shin*. *Do* is created with a species of juniper, and *do uchi* is variegated Japanese cypress. Beneath that is *mae oki* of small yellow chrysanthemums. To its left is the fringed pink for *kusa dome*. *Ki dome*, created with sumac, is on the opposite side. Purple gentian is used as *aizashi*.

Rikka: Fukyu no Shin. Vase: Contemporary ceramic. This Fukyu no Shin Rikka with white *shobu* iris is tall and straightforward to give a refreshing atmosphere. This arrangement can be created in the Sugu Shin (*sugu* means "straight") pattern (see page 39). Utilizing the pattern of an off-centered *shin* helps to create a sense of the casualness of summer. *Soe* and *nagashi* are forsythia leaves. *Mikoshi* is spirea. All three positions create a sense of movement. White blossoms of *deutzia* make up *uke, kusa dome*, and *aizashi*. *Hikae* is hydrangea; *sho shin* is *kakitsubata* iris bud; *do* is Japanese juniper; and *mae oki* and *ki dome* are species of camellia with pink flowers. The yellow chrysanthemums are *do uchi*, and *aizashi* is fringed pinks.

A classic Rikka arrangement in the Sunamono style. This classic Rikka in the Sunamono category (see page 23) was created during the same period as the classic Rikka arrangement in the Sugu Shin style shown on page 40, and used the same labor-intensive processes. Because skilled carpentry is required to make the parts, craftsmen were often hired to make them from the Ikebana artist's sketches. A craftsman, and sometimes the Ikebana artist, would go into the forest and look for pine branches with unique bends and then eventually reassemble them in unique formations. Traditional Ikebana arrangers are required to obtain a diploma of a certain rank to arrange this Rikka. When an artist reaches this level of proficiency, a red lacquered board is placed on the ornate table, underneath the cast bronze *suiban*. This arrangement and the elaborate stand indicate the rank of the artist. During the early sixties, when I was writing the original edition of this book, I was not a member of this highest rank; however, the elders of the Ryusei School who had helped and guided me to create this arrangement offered to allow this format to be used for the sake of publication. The arrangements that follow illustrate different varieties of the Sunamono category.

Rikka: Sunamono in Futa Kabu style. Vase: Typical Sunamono cast bronze with a Chinese motif. This is another Futa Kabu arrangement in Sunamono. Although classic Ikebana has fundamental patterns to follow, there is greater creative freedom when an artist can find unusual lines in the materials on hand. In this arrangement, the *shin* and *nagashi* are pine branches. Comparing this arrangement with the previous one, there are no sweeping lines of *ichi-no-eda* to extend to the right, but the *ichi-no-eda* now turns inward because the basic pattern calls for an *ichi-no-eda*. This pine branch has unique natural bends or curves, and the artist's creative solution here was to leave the *ichi-no-eda* in the reverse direction, or *gyaku*. For this reason, *soe*, which is the quince, is made to be larger than usual. (As has been noted, Rikka is not fixed but allows a certain amount of flexibility to achieve a good design.) The sharp bend in the *shin* pine branch mirrors the *nagashi* branch. *Nagashi* starts to go up and then turns down. These pine branches in movement are almost like contemporary calligraphic brush strokes, sweeping right to left. *Hikae* is bare weathered wood, and the bundles of pine needles serve as *sho shin* for the right-hand unit. To the left is autumnal sumac, which forms *mikoshi*. The height of the sumac is limited, so it will not cross lines with *ichi-no-eda*. *Do* and *mae oki* are formed of boxwood. The pink chrysanthemums placed between *do* and *mae oki* are *iro kiri*. To the right, yellow chrysanthemums in front serve as *kusa dome*. On the right-hand side, a yellow coxcomb next to *sho shin* serves as *aizashi*. On the left-side unit, *sho shin* is the coxcomb, *do* is juniper, and *mae oki* is variegated euonymus. Immediately above, tight evergreen leaves form *iro kiri*. To the left of *iro kiri*, the quince is *hikae*, and underneath, another juniper species serves as *ki dome*. Next to the coxcomb is light-colored weathered wood that serves to counterbalance the right-hand *hikae* of dark weathered wood.

Rikka: Sunamono in a right-hand pattern. Vase: Cast bronze with a Chinese motif and elephant-trunk handles. The main plant in this Sunamono arrangement is a species of aged juniper. The *shin* branch that comes with a large branch extending to the right, as in this example, is unique to Sunamono compositions. This is called the *ichi-no-eda* of *shin*, which means that it is the number one branch of *shin*. The quince branch underneath is *soe*. To balance with the branch above, *soe* becomes much smaller. In this arrangement, the *nagashi* unit and *uke* unit come out of one branch on the left-hand side. On the opposite right-hand bottom, a piece of *shari boku*, or weathered wood, is used as *hikae*. *Sho shin* is at the center and is young pine. To the right-hand side, the euonymus borrows the *shin line* to form *uchi zoe*. To the left of *sho shin*, quince functions as *mikoshi*. *Do* is a species of juniper, and, underneath the juniper, leaves of variegated Skimmia japonica serve as *mae oki*. To its left is *ki dome* formed with sumac. *Kusa dome* is pink gentians.

Rikka: Sunamono in Futa Kabu style. Vase: Cast bronze with a Chinese motif and elephant-trunk handles. Dividing one arrangement into two separate units is commonly known as Futa Kabu (*futa* means "two"; *kabu* means "stalk" or "trunk"). Between the left and right units, one should be able to pass one flat hand with the palm on edge. Futa Kabu in Rikka is the ultimate luxury in Ikebana art. Another type of juniper species with sweeping lines to the right forms the *ichi-no-eda* of *shin*. On the left unit, *nagashi* extends to the left. *Shin*, *ichi-no-eda*, and *nagashi* all consist of the same species of juniper. On the right-hand unit, from the top: fasciated willow functions as *mikoshi*; underneath, the bundles of pine needles are *sho shin*; to the right of the main *shin* branch are ilex berries, which also function as *mikoshi*; underneath the berries is weathered wood for *hikae*; below that is pink gentian for *kusa dome*. *Do* is formed from the same juniper species, and small bits of limb from the main branch show through do, for *do uchi*. Underneath all the material are camellia leaves for *mae oki*. On the left-hand unit, *sho shin* is coxcomb. *Do* is variegated cypress, and underneath it are sumac leaves for *mae oki*. Left *ki dome* is a tight bud of quince. Above *nagashi*, the weathered wood branches function as *uke* for the left-hand unit. Therefore, for the sake of balance, in this Futa Kabu Sunamono, there are two *uke*.

The Seika Style

Seika developed from Rikka into a much more simplified form. Selected from the original nine yaku eda of Rikka, shin, soe, and uke became the main formation for the Seika style. In Seika, the three positions are called shin, soe, and taisaki; together they form an asymmetrical or scalene triangle. The term taisaki means "tip" and is used only in Seika. As in Rikka, Seika arrangements are also erected from the center of the flower vase.

There are three basic styles of Seika: the narrow, or shin, style (formal); the slightly wider soe style (semiformal); and the so, or greater curvature, style (informal). The style selected for an arrangement depends upon the type of floral materials available. Using seasonal flowers also makes the combination of the floral materials and arrangements much freer. The three diagrams of half-circles with graph lines on page 62 show the degrees of curvature necessary (from an imaginary centerline) for the three styles of Seika arrangements—formal, informal, and semiformal.

Historically, Seika arrangements were composed of one material—the exception being the more sumptuous arrangements created for the New Year's celebration, which consisted of three materials. Today the rule has been relaxed, and arrangements made of one, two, or three materials are common. Isshu Ike means that the total arrangement is made from one category of plant (isshu means "one type"; ike means "to arrange"); Nishu Ike (nishu means "two types") is a combination of two different types of plants; Sanshu Ike uses three different types (sanshu means "three types"), and so forth. The purpose of combining different floral material is to create contrast and to bring out each seasonal floral material's characteristic beauty.

Over the years, the original simplicity of Seika changed, and variations such as Niju Ike developed (niju means "double-level arrangements"). To create a Niju Ike arrangement a tall bamboo tube is converted into a two-level vase. There is a top level, and at midpoint a window is cut, into which flowers are inserted, to make the second level. Both levels of the tube are fitted tightly with copper cups because without them the bamboo would split or break from the pressure of the V-shaped kubari. The top holds the main arrangement, with

Left: **Seika: Left-hand pattern in a semiformal Niju Ike arrangement.** Vase: Woven bamboo. In the Seika category, there are a few hanging arrangements. Hence the woven bamboo container used in this arrangement and its manner of display, hanging from a board, could be confused as a Chabana arrangement (see pages 24–25). However, with closer scrutiny it's clear that this is a Seika arrangement. The basic Seika components are honored: the horizontal shin is a bare branch with a leaf on its tip; the soe group has Japanese narcissus in the center; and the taisaki is a camellia branch with its flower serving as tani. In this Seika arrangement, the skill of the artist's handling of the materials is the dominating artistic value. In contrast, in Chabana there should be no attempt to create a style. Also, in this arrangement floral materials do not lean against the rim, one of the characteristics of a Chabana arrangement.

Opposite: **Kenzan Seika, *nejime style*: Bulrush and *kakitsubata* iris.** Vase: Contemporary ceramic suiban. Kakitsubata and shobu irises are among the most lauded of flower and leaf materials for Seika. They are frequently combined with various plants that also grow near water. In this arrangement, around twenty-five bulrush stems form the shin and soe units. Because the bulrush stem is a thin line, even large numbers do not provide enough depth or mass, so one stem is broken at a sharp angle, for artistry and a sense of fullness. This arrangement belongs to the Seika category "by the water," which is discussed on pages 61–93.

Left: **Seika: Left-hand pattern.** Vase: Basket with handle especially designed for tree peonies. In this tree peony *Isshu Ike*, the bare branches of the tree peony form the *shin* and *soe* groups. The tight bud of the peony is the front complement to *shin*, but it is placed much lower than usual, due to the nature of the materials. The middle semi-opened flower, with its leaves, functions as the *soe* front accompaniment. The fully opened flower is *tani*, and leaves to the right serve as *taisaki*. Peonies are considered to be the king or queen of flowering plants. The splendid size and formation of the flower are intensified by having the basket handle serve as a frame for the arrangement.

THE STANDARD STYLE OF SEIKA

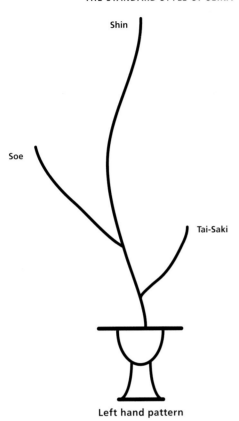

Left hand pattern

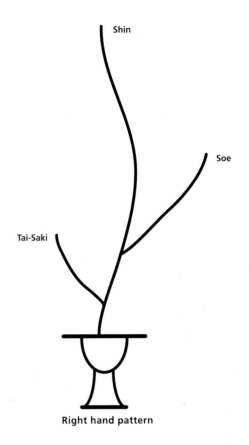

Right hand pattern

branches sweeping sideways, and the window is usually arranged with appropriate seasonal cut flowers to complete a grand view of nature, like an old tree on a cliff sweeping over the valley. As happens in all creative forms, several variations of Niju Ike have been created. When the doors of Japan were opened to the world during the nineteenth century, many new floral materials become available through import. These exotic new flowers were used for Niju Ike, as well as for the classic flower arrangements of Seika.

To successfully create a Seika arrangement, an Ikebana artist must begin by examining and selecting the shin, soe, and taisaki branches from materials that grow naturally. This requires the examiner to have a keen ability to see the potential of the materials. Floral materials that appear at first glance to be quite ordinary become extraordinary when unnecessary parts are removed, and the desired form is created and shaped. The leaves or flowers facing front are called *yang*, and those facing back are called *yin*. Knowing how to balance the yin and yang is very important.

When a Seika arrangement has been successfully created, the strength and beauty of the total creation can deeply move a viewer. The vitality or life force that is manifested by the stylized composition is something one cannot experience from viewing freestyle flower arrangements.

VASES FOR SEIKA

Traditional Seika vases have been made from materials such as bamboo, cast bronze, and ceramic. The major difference between classic and contemporary Seika vases is that in classic Seika, the water basin section had to be strongly constructed, to sustain the pressure of the V-shaped kubari when the pieces were put in place and pressed down (see page 151).

Modern Seika vases are made from a variety of materials because now the floral materials can be held in place with a kenzan. Therefore, the formation and strength of the water basin is no longer of concern. Upon examining these masterpieces in Seika, one can see that a variety of flower vases, from classic to contemporary, have been used. The key point to remember is that in a Seika arrangement, the artistic value of the floral arrangement is still dominant, while in contemporary freestyle, sometimes the artistry of the vase dominates the arrangement.

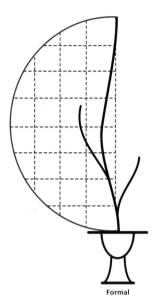

Formal

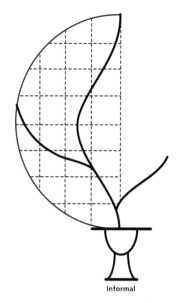

Informal

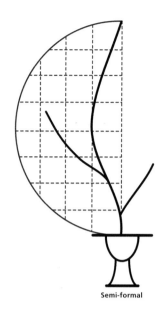

Semi-formal

Formal Seika arrangement

Informal Seika arrangement

Semiformal Seika arrangement

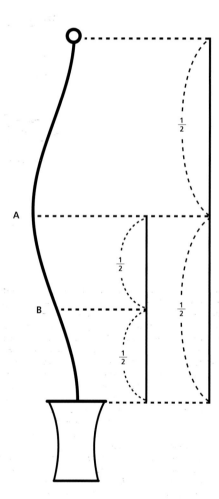

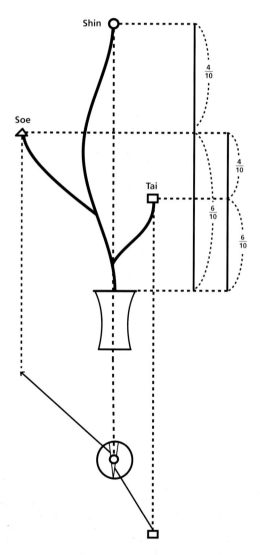

In this diagram, "A" is both the midpoint and the widest part of the curve for the *shin* branch. "B" is a further division of the lower half to show just where the *shin* line should start curving straight down.

This diagram shows the proper proportional relationship among *shin*, *soe*, and *tai*. The tip of *soe* should be $^6/_{10}$ the height of *shin*, and the tip of *tai* should be $^6/_{10}$ of *soe*. The circle below shows how the *kubari* should be placed in the vase. The *soe* branch leans toward the back, and *tai* leans toward the front.

The Nine Basic Positions of Seika

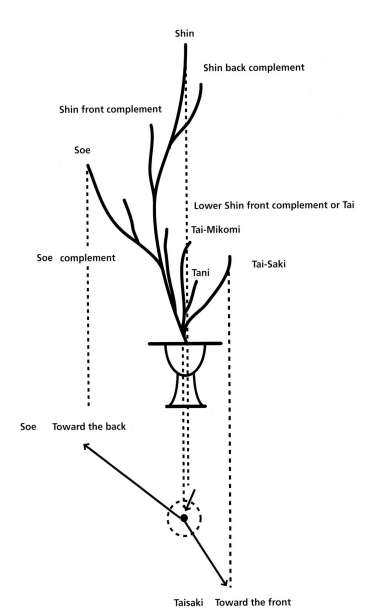

Shin

Shin back complement

Shin front complement

Soe

Lower Shin front complement or Tai

Tai-Mikomi

Soe complement

Tani

Tai-Saki

Soe Toward the back

Taisaki Toward the front

This diagram shows the basic nine positions of Seika and, at the bottom, the directions of the key branches are shown as seen from above the vase rim. The lower dotted circle represents the mouth of the vase. Seika positions developed from the Rikka positions of *shin*, *uke*, and *hikae*. The additional positions eventually developed to make the arrangement more complete—hence the reference to the nine basic positions of Seika. These positions show the placement of materials in an arrangement, whether you're using pine branches, autumnal leaves, flowering trees, or single-plant materials such as aspidistra, chrysanthemums, and so on. The basic form and proportions remain the same, but the materials used bring about astounding differences in the final arrangement, as you will notice in the Seika arrangements that follow.

Seika: Left-hand pattern. Vase: Cast bronze in the style of an ancient Chinese vessel. Lessons in the Seika style of Ikebana commonly begin with the use of aspidistra leaves because they are easy to handle and much can be learned from this broad, flat material. They can be bent to make curves or straightened and stretched rather easily because they are reasonably durable. Many necessary techniques can be learned through this process. In the study of Seika, using aspidistra leaves, it is commonly stated: "Seika training begins with a minimum number of aspidistra leaves and ends with a maximum of leaves when you become a master of that art form." The arrangement shown here of variegated aspidistra is composed of twelve leaves. In Ikebana exhibitions, you may sometimes be awestruck by an arrangement in which the artist has used thirty leaves. Seika is much more simplified than Rikka; therefore, the recognition of the front, or *yang*, and the back, or *yin*, of the leaves is very important. Simply stated, *shin*, *soe*, *taisaki*, and all other positions of the attendant materials must face the sun. So let us pretend the sun is now at the 10:00 or 11:00 clock-face position and angled slightly toward the front. The front, or *yang*, side of the leaf should face the sun. The aspidistra leaf has a central vein in which there is generally a wider side and narrower side. The wide side is *yang*, and the narrow side is *yin*. The selection of *shin*, *soe*, and *taisaki* materials will be based upon this feature. Not only should the leaf face the sun, but the wider side should face the viewer. If we take a tight rosebud as an example, while the bud is tight, we see the back of the flower petal. When the rose is fully opened, the inside, or front side, of the petal is exposed. The fully opened petals, or the *yang* side, surround the center stamen and pistils. Applying this understanding of the laws of nature, aspidistra leaves in a Seika arrangement follow the same dictum, and the *yang* side always faces the center of the grouping.

Above, left: **Seika: Formal Isshu Ike in right-hand pattern.** Vase: Cast iron. This striking simplification of Seika with the use of a camellia branch is often considered the ultimate example of Seika art. A single branch contains the *shin* leaf and its companion leaf for *soe*. The second branch, with a leaf for *taisaki*, combined with the camellia flower, makes up do. Finding a branch with the necessary shape and length, then eliminating all unnecessary elements and stripping it to a bare minimum, does credit to the artist. To create an arrangement such as this, the artist must have sharp and trained eyes, combined with a keen sense of what to eliminate. Such a skill is similar to the ability to use the minimal number of strokes in ink painting. (The vase was designed by the Grandmaster Kasen Yoshimura some fifty years ago.)

Above, right: **Seika: Right-hand pattern.** Vase: Antique cast bronze in the shape of a Chinese wine vessel. This is another formal Seika style using a minimum of materials. Two stalks of Japanese narcissus are very carefully disassembled and reassembled so that the direction of the leaf blades and the position of the flowers are readjusted to the ideal position and then put into the original circular base. Since a characteristic of narcissus leaves is that they tend to spiral, one must carefully select and sometimes forcibly but gently bend them in the direction of the desired design. (Note: Be careful not to over work the blades as this will cause them to became very shiny and lose the natural beauty of their fine white surface.) *Taisaki, do*, and *tani* are all encompassed in one pink quince japonica branch. The arrangement portrays the life force found in narcissus, which in Japan blooms in winter after the first of the year. The smooth narcissus blades contrast with the delicate movement of the branch of quince japonica, yet do not overshadow *shin* and *soe*.

Seika: Hanging arrangement in left-hand pattern. Vase: Bamboo tube cut in the shape of a boat. In Seika arrangements, one can enjoy using unique flower vases, as in this example. The flower arrangement itself gives the effect of mast and sails. There are roughly two styles of boatlike vases: one is a flower vase that is placed on the floor of a *tokonoma*, and the other is a hanging vase. Often the arrangement in the suspended boat suggests a ship in motion. When the boat is arriving, the bow is on the right-hand side, and when it is departing it is on the left-hand side. The horizontal branch (5) in the diagram will sweep down to give the effect of the motion of the wave following the boat. Also in the diagram, *shin* (1) is the mast as the tall point, and *soe* (2) has greater curvature, like a sail as it catches the wind. *Taisaki* is (3), and *tai mikomi* is (4). The key point in a hanging flower vase is that the floral materials must not cross the hanging chain. In this arrangement, the ship is anchored, and the sails are folded down. For this reason, the curvature for *shin* is very slight and almost points straight up, like a pole. The extended *soe* branch is also at a minimum angle. The materials used for the arrangement are fasciated scotch broom combined with small chrysanthemums.

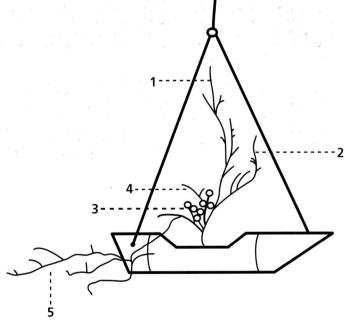

Diagram of a Seika arrangement in a hanging boat vase

Above, left: **Seika: Isshu Ike in a left-hand pattern.** Vase: Cast bronze. The formal Seika arrangement called Isshu Ike is composed of a single kind of plant material. The young flowering *ume* branches exemplify a feeling of "bursting with life." (Formerly *ume* was called flowering plum, but recently the name has been changed to Japanese flowering apricot.) This arrangement is a good example of a basic rule of Seika that a pattern can be adjusted according to the choice of materials. In this arrangement, for the lower part, seasoned ume branches are used, and the *shin* group is accompanied by the new shoots, which usually grow straight out from the aged section of the tree trunk. To enhance this law of nature, the artist makes the *shin* group much taller than the usual standardized height. The selected branches give a wonderful rhythm in line, and from about the center of the right-hand side of *shin*, a branch with limbs attached moves upward and functions as the *shin* back complement, which refers to the treatment of accompaniment. *Soe* is on the left-hand side, and *taisaki* on the bottom right. Using these thin branches is good for practice in Seika arrangements. Because they are easy to bend, one can easily create the standardized curvature for the various positions in a Seika arrangement. Through the experience of arranging materials with a thin line, a student of Ikebana can more easily grasp an under-standing of the overall composition and placement of the materials.

Above, right: **Seika: Right-hand pattern.** Vase: Contemporary ceramic in a traditional style. There is a system of organization in the Japanese arts that is also used in Ikebana. The three fundamental categories are formal (*shin*), semiformal (*gyo*), and informal (*so*). Within these three fundamental categories, additional divisions are formed, such as formal-formal, formal- semiformal and formal-informal. This concept of organization is used for all of the arts: architecture, landscape design, and even Japanese traditional clothing design, to name a few. For example, a black silk kimono for a man who has five white family crests—two on the chest, one on the back, and two on the sleeves at the elbow—is considered formal-formal. Five crests on a grey silk kimono is formal-semiformal, and if the fabric has a certain texture or small patterns with the five family crests, it is formal-informal. The curvature of *shin* determines the arrangement or degree of formality. The curvature of this pine branch is reasonably straight so it is formal-semiformal. This *shin* and its front complement are pine branches. The back complement of *shin* is the curved branch of quince japonica, which gives a distinctive accent to the grouping. The *soe* pine branch also has a front complement of pine, but the back complement is also quince japonica. The Japanese narcissus functions as *taisaki*, *tani*, and *tai mikomi*. This arrangement is called Sanshu Ike, meaning that three different materials are used. The use of more than one kind of material in Seika is a fairly modern innovation. Usually a ceramic vase, or any other kind used for Seika, is lined with a copper cup that fits tightly in the mouth and is generally about four inches deep. (In the photograph, you can see the top edge of a copper cup.) This copper liner helps to protect the rim of the vase. When I was young, with energy to spare, I cracked many a flower vase when forcibly placing in the mouth the V-shaped piece that holds flowers erect.

Opposite: **Seika: Right-hand pattern.** Vase: Cast bronze in the *usubata* (thin plate) category. In this Sanshu Ike, or three-material arrangement, the *shin* group is *Miscanthus zebrinus* (eulalia) grass with white horizontal stripes, which is commonly known as the hawk's feather pattern, or zebra grass. The graceful curving lines of the tips of the grasses contrast with the dynamic movement of the summer sumac that makes up the *soe* group, giving a formal-informal sense to the arrangement. Purple balloon flowers (Chinese bell flower) form the *taisaki* group. Because of the strong movement in *soe*, the selection for the flower vase—a cast bronze in the *usubata* (thin plate) category—is important to visually anchor and stabilize the arrangement.

Above, left: **Seika: Right-hand pattern, "Irregular Left Soe."** Vase: Cast bronze in the style of an ancient Chinese vessel. This striking Seika arrangement in the formal *shin* category is unique. Customarily, *soe* in this pattern should be on the right side of *shin*, but here it is moved to the left-hand side and forms a dramatic bend and sweeping lines. This category is called *chu dan nagashi*, which means "midpoint flowing on the opposite side." Fasciated willow forms the *shin* group, and *soe* in the reverse position is flowering apricot, or *ume*. The *taisaki* group is *hototogisu*, or toad lily (*Tricyrtis*). Please note the placement of *taisaki*, which is now on the right-hand side, since *soe* is on the left-hand side. These flexibilities are allowed if the artist knows how to handle both the composition and the materials. This variation is a good illustration of the fact that classic Ikebana still has great flexibility. It is not rigid. If you have obtained materials that have unusual shapes and lines, the art in ikebana is in how you use the materials, without changing their natural lines, and adjust the rules accordingly.

Above, right: **Seika: Right-hand pattern.** Vase: Antique cast bronze with a Chinese motif. The beautiful sweeping lines of the winter weeping willow without leaves form *shin* in this arrangement. Because the sweeping line on the right-hand side forms a frame over the *soe* position, the volume and length of *soe* can be less. If another thin branch were used on the right-hand side, *soe* could be eliminated. In contrast to the smooth lines of the weeping willow, quince japonica as *taisaki* adds a nice complement. *Shin's* lower front complement is Japanese narcissus. The total arrangement exudes an atmosphere of a calm, sunny day in late winter.

Left: **Seika: Right-hand pattern.** Vase: Contemporary ceramic. This Seika arrangement is given similar treatment to the previous one and creates a sense of formal-informal because it stands upright. Yellow chrysanthemums form the *shin* group, and purple gentians make up the *taisaki* group. Both of these materials are naturally straight with brittle stems, which makes them difficult to bend. For this reason, the placement of the complementary chrysanthemums to the left and right of the main *shin* branch provides a sense of the required curvature. Since the flowers offer very little in the way of curved lines, the young bittersweet vines for the *soe* group give a nice contrast, compensating for the severe verticality with their natural curving lines.

Above, left: **Seika: Right-hand pattern in the formal *shin* category.** Vase: Cast bronze with a Chinese motif and dragon-shaped handles. Fasciated willow and fasciated Scotch broom are very novel types of plant material for Ikebana. They are indigenous to Japan and can be found in many countries. Normally, both materials have long and smooth lines. The fasciated types have an unusual formation of broad, flat stems with new shoots that sprout from their tips. Both willow and scotch broom are reasonably easy to bend, so the arranger can enhance the uniqueness of the branch by adding curvature. *Shin* in this arrangement of fasciated willow is quite active and interesting, with new growth at the tip. Both back and front complement branches have been lowered to enhance the main branch of *shin*. *Soe* is slightly higher, but the ends of the lines are sweeping down, so the spaces between the three—back complement, front complement, and soe—are now given great tension. The white camellia flower with its green leaves as *taisaki* and *tai mikomi* adds life to the total arrangement.

Above, right: **Seika: Right-hand pattern in semiformal style.** Vase: Traditional cast bronze for Seika. Quince japonica in bloom forms the *shin*, *soe*, and *taisaki* groups. From the back, Japanese narcissus forms the *tai mikomi* group. A characteristic of quince japonica is that it is easy to bend and shape; therefore, it is another popular plant type for Ikebana artists, whether it is in bloom or not. In the semiformal Seika style, the curvature for *shin* and *soe* is increased. The back complement for *shin* sweeps out to the left. *Soe's* thick branch comes up to the midway point, and a young branch swings out to the right. In a similar way, the young branch for *taisaki* sweeps out to the left in the lower section, giving the arrangement a feeling of openness and the force of life. The artist has skillfully retained blossoms at the important key points. This arrangement has a wonderful balance of line, mass, and active empty space. Japanese narcissus adds a touch of green and complements the branches of quince.

Above, left: **Seika: Sanshu Ike in right-hand pattern**. Vase: Cast bronze. This serene and yet striking Sanshu Ike is composed of weeping willows spreading out from left to right. This creates a wide, sweeping range in active empty space. The few flowers of quince, as complementary materials for the *shin* and *soe* groups, appear to be minimal, yet they add substantial richness within the context of this simple design. The accompaniment of Japanese narcissus does not detract from the overall sense of simplicity. The cast bronze flower vase gives the arrangement great stability.

Above, right: **Seika: Right-hand pattern in Ura Awase Ike (*ura* means "back"; *awase* means "overlap")**. Vase: Cast bronze in *usubata* style. This arrangement of azaleas is backed with the plant kinbademari, or viburnum, which encompasses a large group of plants with clustered flowers. *Shin*, *soe*, and *taisaki* are composed of the azaleas, and the second set of *shin*, *soe*, and *taisaki* are formed of viburnum, which is overlapped by the azalea. Azaleas are wonderfully suited to Ikebana. During the flowering season, the branches are massed with flowers, and when flowering season is over, the leaves still remain, providing a prolific mass. Eventually the leaves change to dark red or purple. During the flowering season, the blossoms tend to overshadow the leaves, but the bright green leaves enhance the composition and suggest rich growth in early summer. Through skillful choice on the part of the artist, the natural curvature is used for *taisaki*. One must have an intuitively keen sense to detect these qualities in the materials, since azalea branches are quite brittle and will not withstand much bending. The lower ornamentation on the vase is a perfect match for this azalea arrangement.

Below, left and right: Seika: Left-hand and right-hand pattern arrangements. Vase: For the left-hand arrangement, cast bronze styled after a Chinese wine goblet; for the right-hand arrangement, contemporary ceramic. Balloon flowers, also called Chinese bellflowers, are very popular autumnal materials for Ikebana artists. They are one of the seven designated plants for autumn in Japan, known as *aki no nana gusa* (*aki* means "autumn," *nana* means "seven," and *gusa* means "grass/forbs"). Balloon flowers in the bud phase, when the five flower petals are tightly closed, look like little balloons, but eventually they open up into a bell-shaped flower. Variations range from dark purple to lavender but also come in white and pink. The star-shaped blossoms are simple yet elegant. These two arrangements are almost mirror images. Upon close examination, you will notice, especially in the left-hand arrangement, that the *Miscanthus* grass has white horizontal lines; this is hawk's feather pampas grass. The right-hand arrangement (below, right) uses only a couple of blades of *Miscanthus* grass. The *taisaki* group in the left-hand arrangement (below, left) uses the same materials, but the *Miscanthus* grass, with its curvature, enhances the arrangement to complete the autumnal sketch. If the *Miscanthus* grass were eliminated, the right-hand arrangement would fall into the category of Isshu Ike (one kind of plant material). The left-hand pattern is in the Sanshu Ike (three-material) category, with balloon flowers, *Miscanthus* grass, and yellow chrysanthemums.

Below, right: **Seika: Right-hand pattern in semiformal style.** Vase: Cast bronze in *usubata* (plate) style. In this Sanshu Ike, fasciated willow overlaps juniper branches in what is called *awase ike* (*awase* means "overlap"). The two materials, contrasting in both color and texture, are combined for the positions of *shin* and *soe*. In this example, the fasciated willow has dynamic movement, while the juniper branches provide mass. Overlapping enhances the mass and line qualities of the individual materials. In this arrangement, gentian is used for *tai mikomi*, comprising the three different materials used to create this Seika in Sanshu Ike. The unique leg design of the vase adds to the overall effect. One leg of the vase must always be centered in the front. This is true of any three-legged stand.

Below, left: **Seika: Left-hand pattern arrangement.** Vase: Contemporary lacquered vase in an octagonal shape. This is the fundamental form for the left-hand pattern in Seika. In the category of branches, variegated Euonymus japonica is another material that is highly appropriate for the beginning Ikebana arranger. Each branch has a number of attached limbs and abundant foliage, so a beginner has an opportunity to learn how to eliminate unnecessary branches and leaves, and shape the main branches into the desired shape. The required positions for *sin*, *soe*, and *taisaki* are all formed from the euonymus branches. It is important to completely eliminate the leaves from beneath the *shin* back complement, the right side of the main *shin* branch and the left side of the *soe* branch. The final position of *oku nejime*, which is the yellow chrysanthemums, is placed along the lower, bare side of the *shin* branch. *Oku nejime* is used to add depth to an arrangement.

Left: **Seika: Left-hand pattern.** Vase: Cast bronze, styled after a Chinese vessel. This arrangement is a typical example of *Oi Ike* (*oi* means "chase"). *Oi Ike* is an Ikebana style in which a variety of materials, more than those shown here, can be combined in arrangements similar to this example. The hawk's feather, or *Miscanthus zebrinus*, gives graceful curvatures and the basic outline required for a Seika arrangement. The accompanying yellow patrinia gives body or substance to the formation, in addition to enhancing the natural feeling of a meadow scene where such plants often blend together. The secret of using yellow patrinia is to use it while it is very young, before it emits a disagreeable odor. Purple gentian gives a nice accent in the position of *oku nejime*, at the very back of the V-shaped foundation. Usually its function is to give additional depth and a nice accent to the arrangement; in this case, its deep purple color contrasts with the yellow patrinia.

Below, left: **Kenzan Seika: Left-hand pattern.** Vase: White-glazed ceramic in the traditional style, with the characteristic three legs. The arrangement of this *kenzan* Seika of yellow calla lilies is identical to that on page 75. Please compare the two arrangements. The proportion and placement for the required positions are the same. The difference is that, in both blossom and leaves, the yellow calla lilies are much smaller than the white ones. The leaves for this calla species are variegated with white spots, and the overall effect is much less sumptuous than that on page 75. However, it has its own charm in its more diminutive size.

Below, right: **Seika: Left-hand pattern.** Vase: Cast bronze in a classic Seika style. Throughout the centuries, a very popular material for Ikebana arrangements has been flowering cherry branches. There are many varieties of flowering cherry trees—from early blooming to late, and from gorgeous double blossoms to single ones, in colors ranging from light to dark pink. Cherry blossoms have long symbolized samurai because they bloom fully before the leaves appear, and once the blossoms have peaked en masse, they all fall within in a few days, in the prime of life. Many times during peak seasons, I have experienced the twirling and falling of a profusion of petals shaken loose by a gentle breeze, filling my cupped hands in a matter or moments. In this arrangement, cherry blossoms are used for all the components. An artist needs both skillful training and intuitive knowledge to select the proper branches, with limbs attached, and then decide what to eliminate. Just below the main *soe* branch, at the halfway point, one thin branch of blossoms bends down. Generally speaking, in Seika, the flowers are removed from the lower side of the branches for the *soe* and *taisaki* (next to the pine branch) and from the curving inner branch of the *shin* branch. As an exception to this rule, flowering cherry—in this arrangement the little branch that leans out and down from the main *soe* branch—is included to show how the abundance of blossoms weighs it down. The pine branch inserted from behind functions as *tai mikomi*.

Kenzan Seika: Left-hand pattern. Vase: Contemporary ceramic. This arrangement of calla lilies is in the category of *kenzan* Seika because a *kenzan* is used in place of the V-shaped branch piece—the traditional method for holding the materials in place. When the arrangement is completed, the *kenzan* will be covered with smooth pebbles. In a Seika arrangement, the natural characteristics of a plant are recognized and honored. Calla lily blossoms grow straight and tall, and in contrast to the smooth and simply formed blossom and stem, its leaves are quite dramatic in movement. In this arrangement, number 1 is *shin*. While the front shin complement (3)* is generally lower than the back *shin* complement (2), the situation is reversed in this arrangement, as the white blossom *shin* complement is taller than the back complement for *shin*. The leaf point (4) is *soe*, and (5) is the *soe* back complement. Number 6 is the lower front complement or do for *shin*. Number 7 is *taisaki*, and number 8 is *tani*, which means "valley" and refers to the low point in the arrangement. Number 9 is *tai mikomi*.
*In Seika arrangements of calla lilies this is sometimes called the "shoulder."

Above, left: **Seika: Right-hand Pattern in Ume Isshu Ike.** Vase: Cast bronze in *usubata* style. This arrangement is created with flowering Japanese *ume* and makes a nice pair with the previous arrangement. When it stands on its own, however, the focus is on the characteristic dynamism of the branches. Over the centuries, Ikebana students have been told that apricot and peach blossoms are very similar, but that the apricot is masculine because the branches have sharp and rugged angles, and the peach is feminine because the branches have smooth, slender lines with a slight curve. The role of the Ikebana artist is to understand natural law and to enhance the individual characteristics of the floral material on hand. This is a good example of such wisdom, especially in the dynamic movement of the *soe* and *taisaki* units. The artist has lowered the curvature of *shin* to give the effect of strength to the new shoots, which grow straight up. *Soe* and *taisaki* are uniquely formed and ideal for this flowering apricot arrangement. To find such branches for an arrangement is a once-in-a-lifetime experience. The arranger, as an artist, must honor the opportunity to recreate the *chi*, or source of energy, of the aged tree.

Above, right: **Seika: Left-hand pattern in Nishu Ike.** Vase: Antiqued cast bronze in the style of a Chinese wine goblet. The unusual characteristics of plants such as fasciated willow or fasciated Scotch broom make these materials both exciting and challenging for an Ikebana artist. But the artist must have the intuitive skill to study the direction and the individuality of the material, to judge its suitability for the Seika pattern. This arrangement is in the category of *tomo taisaki* (*tomo* means "companion"; *tomo taisaki* means that all three components are of the same material); therefore, the purple gentian will be placed in the flower vase first, and then the *taisaki* unit of fasciated willow will come from behind the flower. The previous example (above, left) is similar in its use of material; however, in this case, the gentian is placed in front and the *taisaki* branch comes from behind.

Opposite: **Seika: Right-hand informal pattern.** Vase: Cast bronze *suiban* with a dragon pattern. A lichen-covered branch of an aged podocarpus tree forms the *shin, soe,* and *taisaki* positions. The addition of bittersweet vines provides an atmosphere of being deep in the mountains. Yellow chrysanthemums function as *nejime*. This arrangement belongs to a category of *tomo taisaki*, so the flowers are in the front.

Seika: Left-hand pattern. Vase: Contemporary ceramic. Japanese apricot branches (for many years known as *ume* plum) covered with lichen show the age of the tree. Japanese apricot trees are hardwoods and therefore cannot be bent and shaped. The two new shoots to the right of the main *shin* branch form a very smooth line and follow the line of *shin*. This addition provides the combination of aged wisdom with the strength of new life. Traditional Japanese New Year celebrations commonly use the pine as a symbol for unchanging happiness and longevity, and the flowering apricot for its bravery in blooming so early in the year, and for the wonderful fragrance it provides, even from under the snow. The red camellia flower with its green leaves takes the position of *oku nejime* to give a nice addition of color.

Seika: Left-hand informal pattern in Isshu Ike. Vase: Cast bronze *suiban* with a Chinese motif. There is a classic custom that permits Isshu Ike (one-material arrangements) made with cherry blossoms to use another type of plant to enhance the main material. This custom is an exception to the usual one-material rule for Isshu Ike. The informal category in Seika has maximum curvature that makes the openings between the three main positions wide. This is characteristic of an informal arrangement in a *suiban* (*sui* means "water"; *ban* or *bon* means "tray"). Because of the size and angle of the branches, an extremely large *kenzan* or a *hako kubari* (*hako* means "box," and *kubari* means "divided") is used. The *hako kubari* is unique to the Ryusei School. An oblong wooden box is nailed onto a foundation that fits exactly into the vase. The oblong box has slots into which plates of thick copper can be inserted. These spaces are adjustable to accommodate the thickness of the branches. When the arrangement is completed, the base is covered with smooth pebbles to cover the mechanism and provide an anchoring effect. In this Seika, a thick branch has been added for stability, to supply an accompanying branch for *soe*, and to provide dynamism to the arrangement. At the midpoint of *soe*, as a rule, a small twig branches out. It is said that the function of the twig is to show the weight of abundant flowers, which causes it to droop. A pine branch is placed in the position of *tai mikomi*, and the poetic name of a distant mountain is given to the pine. This companionship of pine and cherry is also a basic rule.

Above, left: **Seika: Informal arrangement in Sanshu Ike.** Vase: *Suiban* in cast bronze. Bamboo, quince japonica, and white camellias make up the three materials used for this arrangement. As a member of the grass family, bamboo as *shin* is placed in the very front. Quince as *soe* and camellia as *taisaki* come from behind. Because bamboo of this size is so straight, it is necessary to retain the sweeping lines of the branches. The branch placement for the quince, *soe* on the left-hand side, is therefore treated lightly. The *taisaki* unit of white camellia flower is placed close to the center, to break the monotony of the straight bamboo. Because it is difficult to retain freshness in bamboo leaves, the top few joint seals are commonly broken and filled with warm salt water.

Above, right: **Seika: A very formal pattern to celebrate the New Year.** Vase: Classic cast bronze in the *usubata* style. Pine, flowering Japanese apricot, and bamboo form a combination that is time-honored in Asia. A Tang dynasty poem names them as the three friends of winter. In Japan the three branches are customarily used in Ikebana arrangements to celebrate the New Year, so this arrangement is considered one of the most formal in composition. The plant materials are always placed upright in a regal vase, as shown in this example. Vases such as a *suiban*, a double bamboo, or a hanging vase are not allowed. From earliest times, the "three brothers" always formed a unit and were arranged in Seika style for the New Year arrangement. Also, following tradition, the rule was that the forbs/grass category was always placed in the very front, and the category of trees, even with blossoms, was placed behind. Therefore, that same ruling applies in this formal arrangement, and the bamboo, the prince of grasses, is placed in front of the flowering apricot, known as the prince of flowering trees, followed by the pine, which is the prince of evergreens. The lichen-covered apricot branch provides contrast with the shoots for *taisaki* along the *shin* line of the pine tree. The aged pine forms *shin* and *soe*. The bamboo sweeping to the left is characteristic of this formal arrangement, and it can be said that this influence comes from the *uke* position in Rikka, whose purpose is to create a balance in the overall arrangement. In this case, the bamboo is used only because of the formality of the occasion. When materials the size of this stalk of bamboo are placed at the front of a flower vase, the common V-shaped holder cannot possibly hold them. Therefore, an *izutsu kubari* must be used (see the diagram on page 81). This makes it much easier to stabilize the thick bamboo. This *izutsu kubari* is reserved solely for very formal styles of arrangement.

Opposite: **Seika: Left-hand pattern in a classic formal-semiformal arrangement.** Vase: Diamond-shaped flower vase with a Chinese motif. Bamboo and white camellia form this Nishu Ike (*nishu* means "two types"), which is similar to the arrangements shown on this page, where the pine forms both *shin* and *soe*. In this arrangement, the bamboo forms both *shin* and *soe*. Therefore, within the classic formal category, this becomes a semiformal arrangement. Camellia is used for both *taisaki* and *tai mikomi*. The simplicity of this arrangement balances well with the ornate vase. This arrangement also uses an *izutsu kubari* to stabilize the large bamboo branch (see page 81 for a diagram of an *izutsu kubari*).

THE IZUTSU KUBARI: A SPECIAL FORM FOR PLACING MATERIALS IN A FORMAL ARRANGEMENT

To erect and hold in place such materials as thick bamboo, the V-shaped branch section used for flowers will not work. For another system, see the diagram below. Within the circular inner surface of the vase, a box form is created with branch pieces. The width of the frame is determined by the size of the bamboo.

Finally, when all of the materials are in place, the back parallel piece will be forcibly put in to hold all the materials in the box frame. This system is considered to be the most formal category of Seika technique.

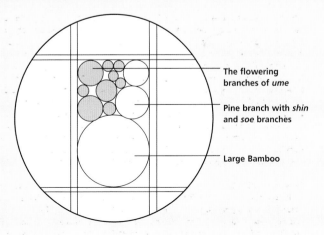

The flowering branches of *ume*

Pine branch with *shin* and *soe* branches

Large Bamboo

Above, left: **Seika: Right-hand pattern.** Vase: One-level bamboo tube. Quince japonica is arranged in an Isshu Ike style. This type of flower vase requires that certain adjustments be made in the basic design. For instance, in a bamboo tube vase, *soe* is usually placed about forty degrees behind *shin* and then brought forward to the usual angle. In addition, the *taisaki* group must remain in the open window of the flower vase. Therefore, the tip of *taisaki* goes up, instead of coming forward. Since this type of flower vase was created in the latter days of Ikebana history, Seika artists were challenged to find a way to break away from the monotony of the usual Seika pattern.

Above, right: **Seika: Right-hand pattern.** Vase: Two-level bamboo tube. This Niju Ike (two-level bamboo tube vase arrangement) is composed of Japanese flowering dogwood and quince japonica. In the previous examples of Seika, the components of *shin*, *soe*, and *taisaki* all appear to have come from one stalk. This unusual arrangement is placed in a two-level bamboo flower vase, a type exclusive to Seika. Previous arrangements are similar in appearance but are on one level. In this work, the *taisaki* group has been separated from the *shin* and *soe* group and moved to the upper level. The arrangement of the *shin* and *soe* group with a slight suggestion of *taisaki* is similar to previous arrangements of quince japonica. Closer examination of the *taisaki* section within the open window shows that it is taller and gives a suggestion of *tani*, one of the nine basic positions of Seika, with a cluster of dogwood flowers to strengthen the hint of *taisaki*, though it is still treated lightly. The upper-level *taisaki* group of quince clearly show the *tani* of flowers. This top arrangement is novel in concept because *shin* is shifted to the horizontal position to the left, and *soe* goes straight up, with *taisaki* on the right. The *taisaki* unit on top creates its own complete unit in minimal form, which makes it a semiformal arrangement. Because the *taisaki* unit is on the top level, it is minimized o shift the major emphasis to the lower *shin* and *soe* unit.

Above, left: **Seika: Left-hand pattern in informal Niju Ike tomo *taisaki***. Vase: Bamboo tube with two water basins. Compare this arrangement to the previous one. The material remains the same, but the sumac comes from a different region, so the color of the leaves provides an autumnal effect. The lines of the branch are much stronger in character. The *taisaki* unit extends out to the proper length, so the balloon flower stays within the framework of the open window. White gentians in the upper arrangement function as *tai mikomi*. The two arrangements are of sumac, yet the emotional feelings they evoke are different. A comparison of the left- and right-hand patterns is also interesting.

Above, right: **Seika: Informal pattern in Niju Ike.** Vase: Bamboo tube with two water holders. The exciting curve of the extended *shin* branch to the left replicates a sketch of a mountain scene with aged tree branches sweeping over a valley. Often such compositions are seen in Chinese, Korean, and Japanese landscape paintings. In the diagram on page 38, the numbers 1 to 4 form the *shin* unit; 5, 6, 7, and 8 form the *soe* unit; and 9 to 11 form the *taisaki* unit. In this arrangement, the *shin* and *soe* units have switched places. The *shin* unit is now horizontal, which puts this in the category of a semiformal Seika arrangement. In the previous formal arrangements in two-level bamboo vases, there is a miniature arrangement in the window, complete with units of *shin*, *soe*, and *tai*.

Seika: Informal left-hand pattern. Vase: Two stacked wooden buckets lined with copper, each styled after a well bucket. This unique flower container consists of two vases styled after old-fashioned, deep well buckets. The use of this type of container evokes a nostalgic feeling for the countryside. One bucket is placed straight, and the other is angled. *Shin*, *soe*, and *taisaki* units are summer sumac, with purple gentian as *oku nejime*. The fringed pink on the lower right-hand side, however, is a small *shin*, *soe*, *taisaki* arrangement. It is arranged in the window of the bamboo Niju Ike and functions to counterbalance the upper part of the arrangement. This arrangement brings to mind the famous *haiku* by the Edo-period poet Chiyo-Ni, translated here:

> *The morning glory.*
> *Twined round my well bucket,*
> *I beg for water.*

Left: **Seika: Right-hand pattern, informal Niju Ike in tomo *taisaki* arrangement.** Vase: Bamboo tube with two water holders. In this arrangement, the *shin*, *soe*, and *taisaki* units are formed from the sumac, and the pink chrysanthemums are *tai mikomi*. In the window opening, the yellow chrysanthemum "*shin*" unit—formed of *soe* and *taisaki*—extends out from the window frame. This gives balance and adds mass, since the upper *shin* branch is rather light in weight. Because of the treatment of the yellow chrysanthemums, the *taisaki* group of sumac on the upper level is minimal. Note that the vase is similar to the others, but is much thinner and taller.

Left: **Seika: Informal arrangement.** Vase: Cast bronze hanging full moon. When this cast bronze vase is used as a hanging full moon, the arrangement is informal, but if it is placed on a table, as a half-moon vase, the arrangement is in the semiformal category of Seika because the chain will no longer interfere with the arrangement. In this full-moon hanging arrangement, the patterns of *shin*, *soe*, and *taisaki* are similar to the top part of a Niju Ike (see page 84), the double arrangement in the bamboo tube vase. *Shin*, *soe*, and *taisaki* are azaleas. The *tai mikomi* is Japanese maple.

Right: **Seika: Semiformal arrangement.** Vase: Cast Bronze crescent-moon flower. If a crescent-moon shaped flower vase is placed on a table or *tokonoma*, eliminating the hanging *chin*, the *shin* and *soe* units can be placed upright from the opening of the flower vase. However, due to the formation of the vase, the *taisaki* unit is somewhat restrained. Small lilies are used for *oku nejime*. *Shin*, *soe*, and *taisaki* are Japanese witch hazel. To the right, on the *soe* branch, a single limb extends out, helping to give an overall balance to the design, in relation to the unusual shape of the flower vase.

Left: **Seika: Informal arrangement.** Vase: Cast bronze hanging full moon. The flowering spirea forms the units of *shin* and *taisaki*. *Soe*, in this case, is the lily buds in the center. The extended horizontal branch of spirea gives the arrangement a more open and relaxed atmosphere.

BY THE WATER

The following several arrangements are a study of the four seasons, arranged with the Japanese *kakitsubata* and *shobu* iris. In both Seika and Rikka, the combination of kakitsubata and shobu iris is a favorite of Ikebana artists. Kakitsubata, with their deep purple flowers and rich green leaves, are among the most beautiful in the category of the iris family. They are considered symbolic of feminine beauty.

Hagumi for Kakitsubata and Shobu Iris

Hagumi means "leaf assembly" (*ha* means "leaf," and *gumi* means "assembling").

When three kakitsubata leaves are reassembled, the longest leaf is in the front, the mid-length is placed next, and the shortest is in between, peeking through, as seen in groupings 1 and 3 in the diagram below. The three-leaf unit is generally placed in the very front of the total group of leaves.

The shobo iris flower comes in many color varieties because of the many hybrids. They grow much taller than kakitsubata and are therefore considered to be masculine flowers. When the three shobu leaves are assembled as a unit, as in group 3, the center leaf will be the longest. It can also be used for the very front of the individual unit.

During the process of arranging, you will use seven to nine units of reassembled leaves. All of the leaf units should consist of two leaves, as in group 2, with the exception of the three-leaf combination at the very front. The way to tell the front and back of the leaf is to hold the end of the leaf blade so it is close to a straight horizontal line. If you do indeed have the top facing up, when you bend the tip, the blade will form a smooth bend. If you have the backside on the top, it will naturally bend down and form wavy lines. When you reassemble the unit, the flower is in the center and all of the front sides of the blades must face toward that center.

When you reassemble, where two leaves overlap toward the center, remove the hairlike structures wherever there is an overlap: Place the leaf down on your worktable and use your wet fingers or wet facial tissue to forcibly wipe the surface clean of the "hairs." Then dip the two or three leaves that are to be arranged together in water. The water will function as an adhesive and hold the unit together.

When arranging the leaves, avoid using leaves of the same height.

THE KABU WAKE AND TOBI NEJIME STYLES

Both the terms Kabu Wake and Tobi Nejime mean that there is a separation in an arrangement (*kabu* means "stalk," and *wake* means "divide"; *tobi* means "jump," and *nejime* means "complementary taisaki"). Kabu Wake is used to refer to arrangements made with iris, and Tobi Nejime refers to all other divided arrangements in which different materials are used for the separate units. There is always a larger and more dominant part that is the original shin unit, and a smaller unit that is the taisaki unit. The two units combine to create a total arrangement, but each unit forms a completed arrangement, while being a complement to the other.

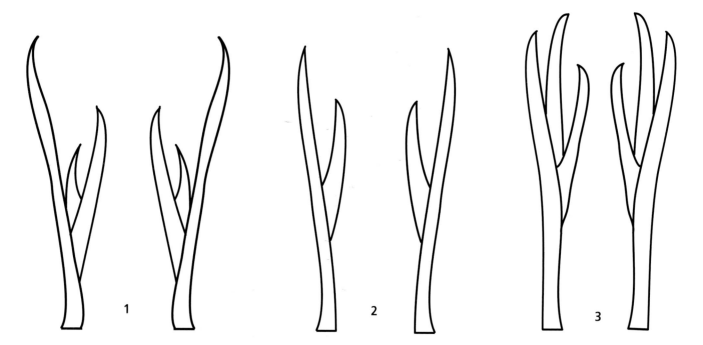

Above: *Kakitsubata* leaves in groupings of two- and three-leaf units. Three-leaf units are generally placed at the front of a group of leaves.

Right: **Kenza Seika: *Kakitsubata* iris in a spring arrangement.** Vase: Contemporary ceramic in the *usubata* style. Full iris leaves in an arrangement, with flowers that are lower than the tips of the blades, show that it is early in the flowering season, which means that the arrangement is in the spring category. The blossoms hold the position of the accompanying *shin, soe,* and *tai,* and the blades with their smooth lines complete *shin, soe,* and *tai.* While the leaves are tender in the early flowering season, they are difficult to shape; therefore, as in previous arrangements, the leaves are quite natural and upright with slight curvatures. As the season progresses, the blades become firmer and can be bent and adjusted to enhance the desired curvature. The *shin* flower is in full bloom, instead of a tight bud as in the previous arrangement.

Above, left and right: **Two informal arrangements of _kakitsubata_ iris for late spring, in Isshu Ike arrangements.** Vase: For the arrangement above (left), Chinese cast bronze _suiban_ with dragon patterns and elephant truck handles; for the arrangement above (right), white-glaze ceramic porcelain _suiban_. When a _suiban_ vase is used, the arrangement is considered to be in the informal category of Seika, although the formation of iris is quite upright and formal in style. The old rule of thumb, based on the desire to create organized beauty in Ikebana, is that _shobu_ irises are masculine, and _kakitsubata_ irises are feminine. _Shobu_ iris can be seen in the Rikka discussion (page 43). The _shobu_ iris is much taller and straighter than the _kakitsubata_ iris and has leaves that are stiff and sword-like. The narrow stiff blades are difficult to bend and shape. The flowers of the _kakitsubata_ iris are much more petite than those of _shobu_. _Kakitsubata_ leaves are wider, smoother, and easier for shaping into curving lines. Because the characteristics of the two irises are dissimilar, the arranger will treat them differently. However, the treatment is the same in the way leaf blades are assembled. All iris leaf blades have the characteristic that the tips bend toward the individual unit or grouping. The rule for reassembling leaf blades is: three leaves for _shin_ and _shin_ back complement; two leaves for _shin_ front complement; two leaves for _soe_; two leaves for _soe_ complement; three leaves for _taisaki_; two leaves for _tani_; two leaves for _tai mikomi_, and flowers for each group.

Left: **Kenza Seika: A summer arrangement of _kakitsubata_.** Vase: Contemporary _suiban_. Compared to the previous example, the flower buds now stand above the leaf blades as _shin_. It is interesting that this arrangement is composed entirely of buds that will open in a couple of days. The anticipation of the fully opened blossoms helps to suggest a cool early morning in summer. The slightly opened bud is now in the position of _mae ashirai_, or front complement of _shin_. Both _soe_ and its front complement are tight buds, and its back complement is a leaf blade. _Tani_ is a semi-opened blossom. Leaf blades for the _shin_ back complement and _taisaki_ have greater curvature, which is a sign of summer and also enhances the required curved lines. The stems of blossoms have the least curvature. The rule for reassembling leaf blades has been applied here. The blade for _taisaki_ in front has the largest curvature. The tips of the two short blades in _taisaki_ face each other to make up the unit. (_Note:_ When an artist assembles iris leaves, one leaf should always be shorter than the other, yet within the unit, the tips must face each other.)

Above, left: **Seika: Formal autumn arrangement of *kakitsubata*.** Vase: Cast iron in a silk-cocoon shape, with a fitted brass cup. Flowering season has passed, so seed pods are now used with taller leaves that are undergoing seasonal changes. Therefore, the *shin* flower is much smaller, and its back and front complement leaves have yellowing tips. The *soe* seedpods are accompanied by the two units of two leaf blades apiece. The *taisaki* unit has three leaves, one of which is curved, and there is a fully opened late-blooming flower.

Above, right: **Seika: Formal pattern for a winter arrangement of *kakitsubata*.** Vase: Cast bronze in the shape of a Chinese wine goblet. After the lush growth of summer, autumn passes, and by winter, only a few scant leaves remain. In this winter arrangement, a minimal number of leaves have been used. Because of the unusual curves of the *shin* pod stem, the *soe* leaves, which are supposed to be directed to the left back corner, now come forward. Beneath the sweeping lines of *soe*, a tip of a withered leaf is exposed, which serves as *tai mikomi*. The ravages of time have affected the stem of the seed pod that serves as *shin*, and its lower left-hand leaf is the *shin* back complement. The little withered leaf near the center is the front complement. The *soe* unit, in contrast to *shin*, has smooth, curving lines. The long withered leaf in front serves as the lower companion to *shin* and is usually right in front of *shin*, but the unique curve of the pod stem provides interest, so this front companion of *shin* has been moved slightly to the right. This also serves to maintain an overall balance in the *shin* movement. Fresh green leaves form the unit for *taisaki*, with the blossom as *tani*. When withered leaves are used, tip curvature is not easily discernible, so the formation of the withered leaf is the deciding factor.

Left: **Kenzan Seika: Summer arrangement of *kakitsubata*.** Vase: Ceramic *suiban*. This arrangement has three flowers with nine units of leaves. Because this is a summer arrangement, the blossoms rise higher than the leaves. If the materials are available, and the occasion calls for it, the number of blossoms and leaf units can be increased. The number of blossoms used can be one, three, five, or seven—only odd numbers of blossoms will be used. *Kakitsubata* iris leaves have their own characteristic curvature. The flat blade curves naturally slightly toward the left or right. According to the curvatures of the blades on hand, the artist will decide on either a left- or right-hand pattern. *Note:* When *kakitsubata* or *shobu* iris blossoms are fully opened, it is easy to find the front of the blossom: one petal should face the very front. However, when the flower is in bud form, study the front and back of the sepals and find the overlap. When the flower opens, the front petal will open fully from that overlap point, so it would be wise to have the overlap point facing the front.

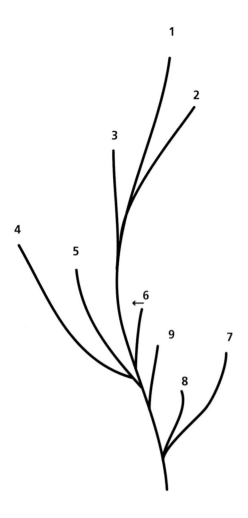

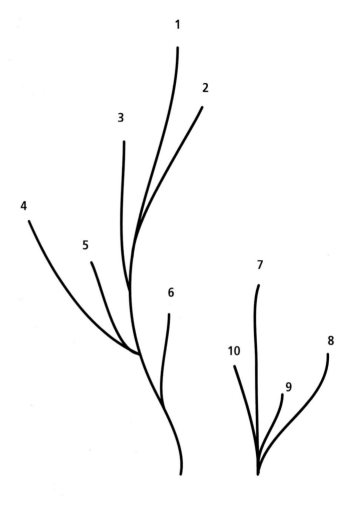

This diagram shows a standard Seika arrangement with the basic nine positions. Compare this to the adjacent diagram for Kabu Wake and Tobi Neijime.

1. *Shin*
2. Back complement for *shin*
3. Front complement for *shin*
4. *Soe*
5. *Soe's* complement
6. *Tai mikomi* (In an arrangement, tai mikomi is placed behind *shin*; however, in this diagram, the line is moved out from behind shin to show its height.)
7. *Taisaki*
8. *Tani*
9. *Do* (additional front complement for *shin*)

This diagram and photograph (opposite) shows a Seika arrangement separated into Kabu Wake and Tobi Nejime. In the Kabu Wake and Tobi Nejime style, the division of positions is one through six and seven through ten, as follows:

1. *Shin*
2. *Shin*: back complement
3. *Shin*: front complement
4. *Soe*
5. *Soe's* complement
6. *Mikomiza*: This means "in place of *tai mikomi*." This variation, which provides a sense of depth, is not always used in the two-division style. There are times when an artist will not wish to interrupt the beauty of a continuous line in the main *shin*, and will not use *mikomiza*.
7. *Tai shin*: This is the *shin* of the second group. *Tai* and the front lower complement of the *shin* of the taller group are the same; however, since it is now separated, the smaller unit creates its own grouping.
8. *Taisaki*
9. *Tani*
10. *Soe za*: Since the right-hand unit is now seen as another grouping, *soe* is to be added. However, this is not a "real *soe*"; *za* means "in the position of." This *soe za* position is reserved only for *kakitsubata* and *shobu* iris arrangements in the two-division styles.

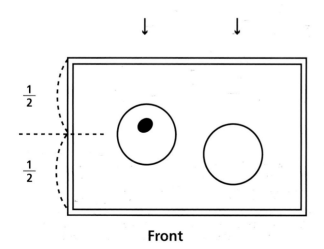

Front

Left: In a rectangular or circular *suiban*, the *kenzan* of the main group is placed halfway between the front and back sides of the vase. This view is from above, looking down on the *suiban*. The two circles represent the placement of the *kenzan*; the dark dot in the circle on the left represents the placement of the dominant *shin* unit.

Seika: Tobi Nejime style Nishu Ike. Vase: Ceramic *suiban*. In this arrangement, the artist uses five *kakitsubata* blossoms that are taller than the seven units of leaf blades. The tallest iris is *shin*, and the bud and leaf to the right serve as the back complement; the front complement is the full blossom in front of the *shin* stem. The flower to the left is *soe*; the sweeping, curved lines of the leaves are the *soe* back complement; and the shortest flower is the *soe* front complement. Since the second, or *nejime*, unit is separate and another kind of material is used, the iris *shin* unit has a three-leaf unit in front to complete the male side of the unit. The female, or right side, is *ko hone* pond lilies (*Nuphar polysepalum*), which are popular Seika materials for the summer season. Because the lily leaves are tightly rolled when young, the placement and height of both the fully opened leaf and tightly rolled leaf must be carefully planned. For this unit, *shin* is the highest opened leaf; *shin* back complement is the other leaf immediately under it, and the flower is the *shin* front complement. Therefore, the leaf in the front complement has been placed slightly lower. *Taisaki* is the far-right open leaf and flower; the rolled leaf is *tani*; the tightly rolled leaf to the left is *soe*; the shorter, tightly rolled leaf is *tai mikomi*.

Above, left: **Seika: A spring arrangement in the Kabu Wake style.** Vase: Contemporary *suiban*-style vase designed by the Ryusei School. The Kabu Wake terminology and tradition have been reserved solely for arrangements made with *shobu* and *kakitsubata* iris, with no blending with other types of plants. The front group in the arrangement forms the *taisaki* and *tani* as a unit. *Tashin*, or the bud, functions almost as *shin* in this right-hand unit. On the left-hand side, the tallest leaf and bud are the main *shin*, and to its right is the back complement; the left leaf forms the front complement. In front of *shin*, the three-leaf unit completes the required positions. The *soe* unit with the buds sweeps to the left between the *soe* and *shin* units. Next to the *soe* bud, the leaves are made shorter with the tip of the peeking leaf as the *soe* back complement, and the front darker leaf as the *soe* front complement. In these separated arrangements, traditionally, the larger side toward the back is called male, and the shorter arrangement in front is called female.

Above, right: **Sanshu Tobi Nejime.** Vase: White contemporary ceramic *suiban*. In contemporary times, as the availability of diverse materials has increased, many variations in Ikebana have developed. Ura Awase style means that *shin* and *soe* are composed of two different kinds of materials, which are then over-lapped. In this arrangement, the concept works well—the *kakitsubata* iris peeks through the bulrush to give a naturalistic and poetic effect. The yellow calla lily, as the female stalk, also grows near water. With the male stalk reasonably erect and straight, the calla lily flower and leaves add a dramatic element. The placement of the *suiban* on two bamboo mats give the suggestion of staggered rafts floating in the coolness of running water.

Above, left: **Sanshu Ike Tobi Nejime.** Vase: Contemporary ceramic Ryusei signature *suiban*. The *shin* and *soe* units are formed from raspberry branches, and fringed pinks function as *tai za* (*tai* means "position," and *za* means "placement"). The *shin* and *soe* units are very bare at the bottom, so the fringed pink is placed to fill in the space. The branch group is the male side, and the *kakitsubata* iris is the female side. Tobi Nejime arrangements are usually a "sketch of a waterside scene." Therefore, the arrangements are usually made up of floral materials that grow near or in the water. If land plants are used, one grouping must be water plants. The space between the two groupings symbolizes the place where fish can swim. Since the iris is the female, shorter side, it should be placed forward. The iris bud takes the position of *tai shin*, which functions as *shin* within the *taisaki* group. In this shorter grouping, the left leaf is *soe*, and the center blades are *taisaki*. Thus, each group has its own *shin*, *soe*, and *taisaki*. However, because the space between the two arrangements must not be compromised, the unit positions in between have been reduced in size and angle.

Above, right: **Seika: Tobi Nejime, two materials for Tobi Nejime: Sanshu Ike.** Vase: Ceramic *suiban*. In contrast to the previous example of *kakitsubata* iris, this *shobu* iris gives an overall impression of strength. The three white buds and their associated leaves form the *shin* unit; two buds with associated leaves form the *soe* unit, and the three leaf unit in front completes the *shobu* iris side. In the Tobi Nejime section, since the materials are land plants, the basic rule is that land materials should not overshadow water plants. As previously mentioned, water plants generally are not mixed with land materials; however, with careful selection by the artist, land plants in the form of purple daisies and sumac of a diminutive size can work well. The movement of the sumac branch gives a nice accent.

Seika: Tobi Nejime. Vase: Contemporary white ceramic *suiban*. Branches of spirea have delicate thin lines. Being somewhat brittle, the branch is difficult to bend and shape, but nature does provide forms that are suitable for various needs. In the *shin* unit, spirea is especially suited to the back complement. Carefully removing the excess leaves exposes the unique qualities of line for *shin*. The lines for *soe* are also carefully developed from the same kind of treatment. The two end branches in *soe* have complementary rhythmical lines and form *soe* and its back complement, *ushiro ashirai*. These complementary pairings are also seen in the leaves of the yellow calla lilies. The placement of small red-orange lilies as *tai mikomi* adds a nice accent. The lilies and spirea are both land plants; therefore, they are placed together in this arrangement.

Seika: Kabu Wake. Vase: Contemporary ceramic *suiban*. This is a very good example of the differences between *shobu* and *kakitsubata* irises. The total height of the *kakitsubata* unit is much smaller and therefore adds to the sense of dominant masculinity in the *shobu* iris. *Kakitsubata* irises always come in deep purple, and the leaves are wider and smoother. On the other hand, the *shobu* iris leaves are narrow and the veins are very strong, so it is very difficult to bend them into gentle curves. It is a wise policy to understand the nature of the plant and work according to its basic characteristics. White *shobu* flowers are used to not compete with *kakitsubata*. However, *shobu* blossoms come in many variations, as the result of generations of hybridization.

From Moribana to Freestyle

Japanese lifestyles have rapidly changed over the last fifty years, and during that time the traditional Japanese concept of architecture has moved to a more Western one. Until recent years, the tokonoma was considered a sacred space, but it is no longer included in modern, Western-based Japanese architecture. Dining and living rooms have open free space, for which the Moribana category of flower arrangement is perfectly suited. The traditional Japanese "main room" was the place to receive guests.

This room was devoid of furniture, and the only decorative aspect was the sliding room divider or fusuma, on which some well-known artist of the time would be commissioned to make a painting. The tokonoma decorations were adjusted to reflect the season or a particular event or occasion. Fine arts, such as a wall hanging and other decorative arts and crafts, were displayed there. The *tokonoma kazari*, or ornamentation, was displayed in a standard way—that is, the trio of hanging scroll, flower arrangement, and art object popularized in the tokonoma.

Today, however, many paintings are hung on the walls, and shelves and cabinets hold necessary items for daily living. Upholstered furniture and tables may furnish the room. The eye level and perspective have changed for the arrangement. Today's open spaces require that Ikebana be viewed from all sides, from 360 degrees. This is totally different from the approach to Ikebana in the past. To be appreciated, Seika must be in a tokonoma and be viewed while sitting on the floor in front of the arrangement. The Moribana category of Ikebana evolved in our contemporary world of free decompartmentalized spaces as a way to create a more three-dimensional, sculptural quality with the use of natural plants.

Left: **Freestyle.** Vase: Contemporary ceramic in yellow glaze. In this freestyle arrangement, the angle of the main line of the flowering peach branches forms a much greater slant than in the previous example. From a perpendicular of 0 degrees, the angle in the formal style is 10 degrees to the left or right. You will notice that the main line of this arrangement is closer to 40 degrees from the perpendicular, placing this somewhat in the semiformal pattern. (See pages 168–83 in "Lessons in Moribana," Part III, for a detailed discussion of the formal, semiformal, and informal styles of Moribana.) After these straight branches have been placed in a more or less fan shape, young eucalyptus branches are inserted to break up the monotony of the straight lines and to follow the fan-shaped pattern. Gerberas and umbels fill in the lower part of the arrangement. The beauty of this arrangement is in the contrast between the straight lines and the gentle curving lines of the eucalyptus. Both are ornamented with flowers or leaves that serve to blend the two different lines. The unique shape and color of the contemporary flower vase helps to harmonize the transition from the yellow umbel, the pink gerberas, and the euonymus to flowering peach.

Opposite: **Freestyle.** Vase: Contemporary suiban with a dark glaze. Freestyle is based on the way a creative artist focuses on the materials at hand, the subject or theme, and the form. Unlike Rikka or Seika, Moribana has no basic fundamental patterns to follow. However, for the beginner, it will help to have some basic knowledge of formation, because one can start from an existing pattern and freely change or adapt it to create one's own Ikebana. In this example, three *shobu* iris with leaves, variegated Japanese euonymus, and fringed pinks are used. The starting point for the arrangement is the Moribana formal category, where the tallest material is *shin*; in this case, the white iris blossom is angled slightly off from the perpendicular, but still very straight. The second and third *shobu* iris are put in place, then the euonymus, which provides movement of line. The fringed pinks give an accent. Upon close examination, you will notice that the heights of the individual materials all differ slightly. Having the main flower at a slight angle creates a wonderful sense of activity on the left-hand side. On the right-hand side, with the exception of one *shobu* iris, it is the active empty space that is to be appreciated.

Moribana, which means "piling up of flowers," focuses on creating volume that can be appreciated from all viewpoints. Flower vases in the past required few variations in pattern, but today contemporary ceramic artists are creating a variety of vases, some more like contemporary sculpture. From a Bauhaus concept of pure simplicity to an emphasis on colors and textures, containers of all kinds have become abundantly available. This great variety of new flower vases has inspired Ikebana artists to create freestyle Ikebana.

To simplify the learning and mastering of Moribana, the formal, semiformal, and informal styles are used as fundamental techniques for beginners. These styles will be briefly touched on in the arrangements that follow. (The formal, semiformal, and informal styles of Moribana will be more fully discussed on pages 166–85 in "Lessons in Moribana." Moribana utilizes kenzan to hold floral materials in a vase.

The floral materials are given proportions from long to short, and angles to determine balance. Consideration is given to seasonal branches, flowers, color combinations, and texture. There are specifics about how to treat given materials. These are considered the basic techniques required for creating an Ikebana arrangement in the Moribana style.

Later in this book, we will go on to freestyle arrangements. Many Ikebana artists have begun to "re-recognize and reevaluate" individual plants and their beauty, a new perspective that has allowed them to create inspired arrangements. This creativity, rooted in the newfound beauty in traditional and nontraditional materials has increased the pleasure to be found in Ikebana.

The next three arrangements are examples of the basic styles of Moribana. The fourth arrangement is a particularly masterful Moribana arrangement. These are the first steps to learn before moving on to create freestyle arrangements.

Above: **Freestyle.** Vase: Ceramic bowl with a dark blue glaze. A branch of forsythia forms the main branch of this arrangement and is angled in an almost horizontal position, which places this in the category of informal Moribana. The peony buds counterbalance the long branch, and yellow chrysanthemums provide an accent to the lower section. Peony leaves cover the *kenzan*.

Opposite: **Freestyle.** Vase: Contemporary glass. In a freestyle arrangement, the starting point is the kinds of materials the arranger has on hand. Choosing from what is available, the arranger must decide which material should be dominant; then, which will follow as subdominant, and so on. In this wisteria arrangement, since the blossoms are clustered, their formation becomes the dominating mass. This contemporary glass vase with its unusual legs enhances the floral materials and becomes a part of the mass. The lines in the iris become secondary and therefore are subdominant. The strength in this arrangement is not in building up mass for its own sake, but in creating breathing space as active space. If you happen to have an abundance of line materials, then you can create lines as the dominant feature. If you have an abundance of materials with flat surfaces or planes, as in beautiful leaves, then they can be the dominating material. The concept of dominant, subdominant and subordinate—large, medium, and small—finds its roots in the Seika category of Ikebana as *shin* (dominant), *soe* (subdominant), and *taisaki* (subordinate). This concept in organization is quite useful in dealing with the visual sense; yet, it can also be applied to the sense of taste. To enhance sweetness, add a little bit of salt; to mellow the taste of salt, add a little sugar. Use this understanding, and do your best to avoid using all materials in the same amounts, in volume or height, and remember that active empty space can be used as one of the ingredients or materials. The organization of freestyle Moribana, as in any form of visual creativity, can provide an unparalleled learning experience. This is a masterful freestyle arrangement. While the light purple of the wisteria is echoed in the dark purple of the *kakitsubata* iris, the green planes of the iris blades provide a contrast in color, texture, and formation. Much can be learned from such an arrangement.

Contemporary Ikebana

Nature and the laws of nature are the foundation for the stylized creative beauty of classic Ikebana, which has been handed down for many generations. The concept and style of classic flower arrangements— such as Rikka and Seika—continue to be fundamental, but modern tastes have led to the use of a variety of materials not previously used in Ikebana.

This exploration of materials has brought a new creative freshness to Ikebana, and with it a fresh interpretation of the classic forms or styles. The creative sensitivity found in contemporary Ikebana arrangements is unparalleled in the art form's long history. This metamorphic change is based upon an artist's creative use of familiar leaves, branches, and flowers to express a personal interpretation of the material. This approach requires an artist to acutely focus on individual elements and discover their unique beauty, which has been overlooked in the past.

For example, let's examine the Western concept of still-life painting, which typically includes a table with a bowl of fruit. The natural form, texture, and color of the fruit contrast with the man-made bowl and table. The different types of elements incorporated in the painting create its effect. Now, however, instead of viewing the composition as a whole, focus on a single element, for instance, the fruit itself. One might concentrate first on the color of a fruit, then on its structure, then its texture, and next imagine its fragrance and taste—and finally reassemble all those aspects to re-create them in a painting. This approach can be found in the paintings of flowers by Georgia O'Keefe or in works by Andy Warhol, for example. In the mid-twentieth century, artists began to go beyond form, to focus on color and texture alone. What at first glance appears to be a monochromatic canvas, painted in black or white, displays upon close scrutiny a variety of brushwork, texture, and divisions. Undoubtedly, readers of this book have experienced such abstract works in fine art museums around the world.

Left: **Japanese narcissus.** Vase: Contemporary ceramic. As part of the New Year celebration, in a traditional *tokonoma* arrangement, it is common to see long weeping willow branches (without leaves) arranged high up, close to the ceiling. These long weeping willow branches—symbols of good luck and fortune—drape down and are tied to make circles here and there. Following that tradition, various kinds of long-leaf materials, such as pampas grass, or narcissus and iris blades, are often tied as circles in contemporary arrangements. However, in this example, perhaps the unique flower vase with its three thin, painted lines inspired the artist to create this stunning arrangement. The narcissus leaves are carefully overlapped and then gently and neatly tied in a knot, then accented with their own blossoms. In its simplicity, this is a dynamic arrangement. If plant materials were not used, this arrangement could be considered a contemporary sculpture.

Opposite: **Freestyle: Spirea and freesia.** Vase: Contemporary ceramic. Spirea has been given the same treatment as in the previous example, providing line and mass for the composition. The freesias have been given a similar treatment, to add line and mass. The orange-red freesias add contrast and liveliness to the composition. Many branches of spirea cross at the top to create mass, which complements the shape of the contemporary flower vase. The center part of the arrangement has been carefully divided to create active empty space. The freesia leaves in the center give a final accent by adding the "plane" element.

Freestyle: Japanese narcissus. Vase: Contemporary square *suiban* made of stoneware. The previously mentioned the "*suiban* without *kenzan*" concept is extended in this composition. Originally, that concept developed around the idea that the various materials could lean against and support each other in order to stay upright. Then eventually Ikebana artists began to make horizontal arrangements. This new movement led to the creation of many new styles in *suiban* vases, such as the one seen in this narcissus arrangement. While unique, the piece is familiar in style to Ikebana enthusiasts. With careful scrutiny, one should notice that the white part of the stalk has been meticulously arranged with the openings of the leaf section lined up, and that from the far left, each leaf stalk has been painstakingly cut to fit in an angle. On the far right, three lines of leaves carefully divide the surface of the water. Thus, the active empty space is highly utilized as a key element in this Ikebana arrangement. The two leaves with yellow-brown tips add a special touch to the arrangement as well.

Above: **Freestyle: Pine.** Vase: Flat ceramic tray with handles. Pine needles can survive in a flower vase without water for a few days. In this arrangement of long green pine needles and short brown pine needles, the aged pine needles are placed on a dish, rather than in a flower vase, and lilies are placed in orchid tubes, which are hidden by the brown needles. Long pine needles are scattered over the entire arrangement. This creative artistic statement suggests that the wisdom and knowledge of generations can lead to the cultivation and flowering of new forms and concepts of beauty. Once the artist's mind is released from the conventions, traditions, and history of an art form, the creative concept reaches another level. Whatever the materials may be—fabric, metal, bamboo, or any others—the end result will be something unique and exciting. Yet, no matter how freed an individual artist is from the traditions of Ikebana art, there is one basic rule for all Ikebana styles: plants require water.

Right: **Freestyle: Spirea and quince japonica.** Vase: Contemporary porcelain. Placed in a contemporary flower vase with a smooth plane surface, the combination of materials makes this a masterful composition. The amazing simplicity of this contemporary Ikebana could not have been created without the artist's rich training and background in classic Ikebana. As a comparison, see the Seika arrangement on page 64, where a single camellia branch was used. This arrangement echoes the classic concept expressed in the Seika arrangement. Here, all the leaves and flowers have been removed from the lower part of the upright spirea branches, to stress the quality of the line. The flowers on the upper end compensate by giving an illusion of stamina and energy to an otherwise bare branch. Quince japonica forms a mass on the lower left-hand side, providing great contrast. Each viewer will interpret this artwork in a personal way. That is the pleasure and strength of contemporary freestyle Ikebana.

Top: **Moribana: Spirea.** The category of plants with thin, flexible, and durable leafy branches, such as spirea and young eucalyptus, can all be treated in a similar way. In this example, a branch of spirea has been shaped to a very natural form, with flowers and leaves draping down gracefully. This spirea branch is very beautiful in itself, but for an arrangement, the artist must decide what type of flowers should be combined with it, and which element of the branch should be the focus. These considerations are the first step to contemporary creative Ikebana.

Above: **Freestyle: Spirea and umbels.** Vase: Iron-glazed contemporary container. This stunning arrangement is also a composition of mass and line. Light-colored flowers form the mass and are supported by the braided lines of their own branches. The iron-glazed contemporar r serves to visually anchor the base. The floral materials are spirea and umbels.

Top: **Moribana: Spirea.** Some of the leaves and flowers from the branches of spirea have been removed to expose the bare branch. This enables the quality of line to be given acute focus. Retaining the flowers at the tips of the individual branches enhances the graceful curvatures and adds weight and mass. The focus and interest are now in the line and mass of the material.

Above: **Freestyle: Spirea.** Vase: White-glazed contemporary ceramic. The concept for this arrangement is quite unique. Young spirea branches with flowers and leaves form the core tower. Spirea branches with all their leaves and blossoms removed make up a skeletal structure that extends from the ends of the angular flower vases, creating a contrast of winter and spring. The L-shaped white-glazed contemporary vases are placed side by side and appear, at first glance, to be one vase. The L-shaped containers allow light to pass through and give a sense of depth to the arrangement.

The book *Shokubutsu No Kao*, written in 1980 by Mr. Kasen Yoshimura, the iemoto, or grandmaster, of the Ryusei School, discusses one of the new movements taking place in contemporary Ikebana. A direct translation of the title is *The Characteristic Face of Plants*, with the subtitle *The New Key to Ikebana Creativity*. In essence, Grandmaster Yoshimura writes, the main materials for Ikebana are plants. Plants are nurtured by nature, are living things, and, in their original form, have color and texture. When an individual who is in a state of total concentration and involvement observes a living plant in its totality and universality, he or she cannot help but be deeply moved. When observing a plant in this spirit, one can recognize "uniqueness" as its essential character, and this awareness forms the core of creative Ikebana. This is what makes modern Ikebana exciting, and at the same time poses the greatest difficulty and challenges. One must surpass and transcend concepts of traditional use and discover a "new face" in the material, and this "new face" is the primary focus of contemporary Ikebana. This viewpoint, first put forth by Grandmaster Yoshimura of the Ryusei School, has now influenced other schools as well.

The Ryusei School annually conducts an Ikebana exhibition on a grand scale in Tokyo. Over five hundred works by selected artists from the various chapters throughout Japan are presented. This exhibition, which is open to the public, includes works by the grandmaster and his teaching staff at the headquarters, whose arrangements range from midsized to large works. The exhibition is divided into two sessions, with many of the art works changed for the second session. Each year, a large space in the exhibition hall is reserved for arrangements of a specific plant that has been selected as the main focus. For example, if the focus plant is pine, each artist will study the plant's formation and unique qualities carefully, from every angle, to make an arrangement. The familiar plant will be arranged in vastly different ways, often bringing surprise, pleasure, and joy to the viewer. New and unique ways to create an arrangement will give visitors, especially Ikebana fans, a new sensitivity to the plant material, a new awareness of its potential—thus paving the way for new approaches and greater creativity when they create their own arrangements.

I have selected works featuring familiar plants as examples for this section, from an enormous array of fine creative works. The readers of this book should be able to easily obtain these familiar floral materials in their natural surroundings or markets. I hope that in these works you will discover new ideas that will release your personal creativity in Ikebana.

Freestyle: Spirea, larkspur, and anemones. Vase: Contemporary blue-gazed *suiban*. This type of *suiban* is one of the officially designed vases for the Ryusei School. The container inspires great creative imagination. Primarily to provide mass to the arrangement, the spirea branches are relatively untouched, except at the bottom. The bare branches in the lower part form a frame for the light blue larkspur. The flowers at the bottom are purple anemones and function as a transition, blending the upper arrangement with the *suiban*. Mass is the dominating theme in this composition.

Left: **Freestyle: Pine.** Vase: Contemporary ceramic. A bundle of rice stalks is centered in this contemporary white ceramic vase as if it were a candle with a red torch, which is simulated with a "lobster claw," or Heliconia, spike. The entire arrangement is ornamented with a pine branch.

Bottom, left: **Freestyle: Spirea.** Vase: Contemporary white porcelain vase. This striking composition of spirea and red anemones arranged in a contemporary vase is tightly fitted with white Styrofoam™ to hold the plant materials in place. The spirea branches and anemones are carefully inserted between the inner surface of the bowl and the Styrofoam—therefore, all of the plant materials come out from the edge. The front group goes from right to left, and the back group moves from left to right, forming a single mass, yet the feeling of movement is clear. One red anemone provides a striking and clever accent by covering the left-hand spirea branch stems. The white spirea, red anemones, and white vase form a beautiful contrast.

Right: **Freestyle: Pine.** Vase: Contemporary *suiban* made with sheet metal. For centuries, the pine has held the honored position of the main branch in Rikka and Seika arrangements. If the great Ikebana masters of the seventeenth and eighteenth centuries could see this contemporary pine arrangement, imagine what they might say about it! This pine is a species of *dai o-sho* (*dai* means "big," *o* means "king," and *sho* means "pine") and is considered the best of the long-needle pines. It is erected as a freestanding arrangement in this contemporary vase, using a concept or technique of making an arrangement in a *suiban* without a *kenzan*. The sides of the *suiban* are angled sharply inward so that plant materials can lean against and support each other. This vase is specially created so that stems bearing the weight of the plant will push against the corners of the vase. This concept was developed in the 1980s by the Ryusei School and is commonly known as "the *suiban* arrangement without the use of a *kenzan*." Since then, this new approach has become widely accepted throughout Japan. This stunning arrangement uses the technique "without *kenzan*" but moves one step further by using metal rings to bind the pine branches together in a couple of places. The idea of using metal or other materials to bind the materials together is very unusual. The metal rings echo the metal flower vase. The red tropical flower is used for accent. Note: Using a Suiban without Kenzan. To arrange without the use of a *kenzan*, the arranger must pay special attention to the "legs" of the plant. They must be cut at an angle and positioned so that the plant can support itself. In addition, for aesthetic reasons, the creator must pay close attention to where and how "the line form" comes out from the vase. Visually, this is the important challenge. In other styles of arrangement, such as Nageire, or when using a *kenzan*, the leg or stems of the plant are generally not exposed and, therefore, are not of great concern.

Left: **Freestyle: Pine.** Vase: Contemporary stoneware with a white glaze. A common practice in landscaping or Ikebana is to remove aged leaves or bug-eaten leaves. However, when arranging aspidistra in Ikebana, especially in Seika, the second leaf from the front, which is in the position of *tani*, is deliberately torn to give a worm-eaten effect. See the photograph on page 164. Many other plants have been given a similar treatment in Ikebana. When tending to a traditional Japanese garden, a seasoned gardener will take time to painstakingly remove old brown pine needles. In this striking design, however, the old brown pine needles are used as the main feature, instead of unique variegated pine needles. You can see the lower part of the white flower vase, but it is mostly covered by needles, in a contrast of green and brown, supported by the bare and textured brown branches in their unique curvature. In addition, there are young rubber-plant leaves, one still a reddish-pink unopened bud, and a branch of flowering quince. The artist's statement could be that of a "creature" representing the planet Earth.

Right: **Freestyle: Japanese Narcissus.** Vase: Contemporary stoneware. The traditional treatment for Japanese narcissus is to show admiration for the smooth, long, slender green leaf blades, not just for the flowers. This attitude and approach apply to most of the flowering materials. For instance, in an American flower market, chrysanthemums and other flowers are sold mainly for the blossom, and the leaves for the most part are missing. In a Japanese market, the leaves are as important as the blossom, and sometimes more important. The size, color, and formation of the leaves often determine the price in Japan. In this arrangement, the artist breaks the usual tradition in the treatment of leaves; an abundance of narcissus leaves are carefully sculpted by bending and folding. The form and composition provide mass and texture, enhanced with lines. An occasional narcissus blossom peeps out to give accent. This handcrafted flower vase is in the shape of a half-circle and enriches the total arrangement. The bending and folding of the leaves do not necessarily suggest a disturbed or depressed state of mind, but somehow give a feeling of hope—among the downward-looking and distressed leaves, flowers peek out.

Left: **Freestyle: Japanese narcissus.** Vase: Contemporary ceramic with a white glaze. Throughout this section on freestyle, or "the characteristic face of plants," many unique and striking contemporary flower vases are introduced, with examples of how they can be used most effectively in arrangements. This arrangement is yet another example of how floral materials and a vase can be combined for a stunning presentation. The lower part of Japanese narcissus has been cut in assorted lengths and angles, then carefully arranged according to height and angle in the platelike container. The color variation is due to the varying height of the pieces from thick to very thin and enhances the uniqueness of the vase. The arrangement is adorned with one leaf blade and one stalk with a flower.

Right: **Freestyle: Pine.** Vase: Contemporary ceramic Vase with a white glaze. In the previous four arrangements, long-needle pine branches were used. In this brilliant creation, short needles were used to provide additional texture, and the composition is accented with one red rose. The artist has made this horizontal arrangement to utilize this uniquely designed flower vase, which allows water to be supplied to the pine branch. This original arrangement is composed of three very common materials.

Freestyle: Maple. Vase: Ceramic *suiban* with a white glaze. An abundance of green maple leaves lean against the bare azalea branches. This is a good example to show how the freestanding technique is carried out. The convoluted mass of sturdy azalea branches is put in place first; several of its branches contact the outside of the *suiban* and serve as a stabilizing factor. The branches of flowering azaleas are added next, then finally, branches of green maple are put in place and partially cover the azalea flowers and bare branches. Please observe the surface of the water. The key point is that the surface of the water is left open to give a sense of lightness to the top-heavy composition. Making arrangements with masses of leaves in Ikebana requires an intuitive sense of the laws of physics. The freestanding branches should be able to sustain their position with a minimum of contact with other materials. To the right of the main maple branches, a couple of branches are actually contacting the rim of the *suiban*, which has a slight inward angle that serves as a brace. Maple leaves very cleverly cover the main branch of the maple that is braced against the rim. On the far right, one small, bare limb ex-tends out, which helps to balance the arrangement. To appreciate the balancing effect of this small limb, cover it with your finger and examine the arrangement's appearance.

Freestyle: Maple. Vase: Contemporary blue-glaze ceramic. Two species of maple branches are overlapped. The thin, reddish, finely-divided leaves create a lacy screen, through which the green-leaf maple and yellow flowers are peeking. This approach in composition is quite poetic, since from earliest times in Japanese literature, the sense of "half-revealed" instead of "fully exposed" has been honored. This concept is commonly known as *yugen*, and it is the essence of Noh drama, as well as *haiku* with their composition of only seventeen syllables. In *haiku*, the poem suggests rather than gives a complete description. The idea, metaphorically expressed, is that beauty can be better appreciated when seen mysteriously, "through the bamboo curtain," than when seen in full view. Technically, with the use of a *kenzan*, this arrangement is in the manner of the basic Moribana style. The front maple plane gives depth to the composition by having a different color and texture than the other maple, and both are enhanced by the use of yellow statice, pink Japanese spirea, dropwort, and hydrangeas. This is a successful work of art in which the basic principles of Moribana are used.

Above: **Freestyle: Maple.** Vase: Contemporary ceramic. Another variety of maple is used in this striking work. This design concept could not be carried out without the use of this unique contemporary flower vase. A plane of the leaves on the right-hand side forms the mass, and, on the left-hand side, bare branches of maple and vines stripped of leaves create a complex series of lines. Simply stated, the plane is dominant, the lines are subdominant, and the flowers are the accent. As can be seen in this work, along with many other examples in this section, many contemporary arrangements are based upon "asymmetrical balance." For example, if this flower vase were placed parallel to the viewer, or coming straight at the viewer, the arrangement would not achieve an asymmetrical balance. Many forms of Japanese art, especially in traditional paintings, are based upon asymmetrical composition.

Right: **Freestyle: Maple.** Vase: Contemporary glass. Maple trees come in many varieties. In recent years, many varieties of Japanese maple have been gaining popularity in the United States. Many of these various Japanese maples have branches and leaves that are lacy in effect. In spring the leaves are a beautiful fresh green, in summer they turn to dark green and provide shade, and in autumn the leaves may turn yellow, orange, or deep scarlet, depending upon the species. Because maples display this seasonal beauty, they are very popular in Japan, but especially so during the autumn season. Many public events are organized as maple-viewing celebrations, which are equal in popularity to the cherry-blossom parties during the spring. It would be impossible to conceive of this striking arrangement without the unique contemporary glass container. The maple branches and leaves are arranged in a fan-shaped manner, sweeping from right to left, leaving an open space underneath the far-left branches. The upper part of the arrangement forms a plane of leaves, while the middle part is made up of fine branch lines. Both are assembled to form fanlike planes and then are coordinated with the flat, planelike vase. The masterful treatment continues in the vase, since one can see through the glass. The lower branches or stems of the plants are customarily not to be seen, but here they are given focus and form a very important part of the arrangement. Using your imagination, remove the upside down V-shaped branch in the vase, which, in actuality, is helping to support the branches. Without the V-shape, the arrangement loses visual strength. Lavender blossoms of delphinium echo the color of the vase and add a subtle uniformity to the total arrangement.

Top: **Freestyle: Camellia.** Vase: Contemporary ceramic bowl. There are two kinds of flower arrangements: One functions as part of the room décor and as an expression of gratitude, or as a celebratory gift of a bouquet. Floral materials in these cases should be made to last as long as possible by changing the water every day. The other form of flower arrangement is intended as a work of art. This striking visual offering, along with many other examples in this book, is in the latter group and was created for artistic purposes. This thick branch of camellia will last for a week or so without a supply of water. The suggestion of water is in the unique shape of the vase, with a few blossoms floating on the surface. This evokes the feeling of offering flowers at a shrine or temple, as was the custom in ancient times. Upon careful examination, you will notice that one twig is in the water with the corkscrew willow and will provide some water for the camellia branch.

Above: **Freestyle: Camellia.** Vase: Contemporary stoneware with a yellow glaze. Camellias, originally imported to Japan from China, are one of the most loved flowers of the winter season. Recently, many hybrids have been created and come in varieties of sizes and colors for the pleasure of all who love flowers. In Japan's mild winters, this is a common plant. Green tea is a member of the camellia family. Camellias have a smooth bark, interesting lines in their branches, and shiny, dark green leaves. It is usually the simple classic form of their blossom that is used in Ikebana. Two vases with the same design are used to make this composition. The right-hand side has more mass, with the flat planes of the camellia leaf, which are punctuated with many tight buds and a few opened blossoms. The emphasis on the left-hand side is on line rather than mass.

Left: **Freestyle: Camellia.** Vase: Contemporary *suiban*. This arrangement uses another classic deep pink camellia. The mass of stamens in their center gives camellia blossoms their characteristic beauty. In hybrids, as the number of petals increases, the stamens get covered and are reduced in size. Camellia leaves are smooth and shiny and are often used as garnish in Japanese cooking. The branches in this arrangement are arranged so that almost all of the leaves face the viewer, which promotes mass, with the flat planes showing. The exposed branches suggest line movement.

Freestyle: Camellia. Vase: Contemporary ceramic bowl. By this time, you must have become aware that in freestyle arrangements, the container plays an important role in the total presentation. In this striking arrangement, the aesthetic importance of the vase is readily apparent. The mass formed by the branch of camellia leaves and blossoms is enhanced by the convoluted line mass of corkscrew willow. Though the mass is off center, because of the strong camellia branch, it is well stabilized. The space between the upper mass and the vase, which is connected by the V-shaped camellia branch, is also very important to the success of the composition.

Freestyle: Eulalia, or *Miscanthus* grass. Vase: Molded ceramic. Flower blossoms are generally used in this type of composition, but in this arrangement, the *Miscanthus* grass is the dominant factor. *Miscanthus* grass comes in many varieties of variegated plants and belongs to the grain family. It is a very popular plant among the Japanese. During the autumn moon-viewing celebrations, *Miscanthus* grass, with its foxtail-like plumes, is displayed with other autumnal fruits as an offering to the full moon. The tail-like plume in Japanese is called *o bana* (*o* means "tail," and *bana* means "flower"); however, in contemporary arrangements, the leaves are more widely used, for their line quality, since the plumes come only at the end of summer, but the graceful leaves are available from spring to fall. This graceful composition of variegated *Miscanthus* grass is like a green fountain. It is accompanied with corkscrew willow to break the monotony of orderly leaf patterns and accented with Japanese barnyard millet, which is placed in the center to add an element of texture.

Above: **Freestyle: *Miscanthus* grass.** Vase: Light-blue porcelain. This is another arrangement that shows the graceful and curving lines of a common variety of *Miscanthus* grass. This arrangement, just as in the previous work, demonstrates a naturalistic use of the plant. However, in this arrangement, additional curves are given to the grass. The rhythmical composition of the lines of the leaves is very carefully constructed. At first sight, the right and left appear to be equal, but upon closer examination, the right has more emphasis. The direction that the pink cosmos blossom at the top faces leads the focus to the other opened blossom and the creative empty space above the grass. The division into many pockets of space created by the leaf lines at the left could be too busy, but being guided to the open space to the right eases the tension.

Opposite: ***Miscanthus* grass.** Vase: Contemporary ceramic with a black glaze. The leaves of variegated *Miscanthus* grass are bent sharply to create multiple angled lines that are then accented at the very top with the deep-pink stems of a species of castor plant with leaf and seeds. (The oil from the castor seeds has medicinal uses.) This appears to be a simple design, yet there are many aspects in its simplicity to appreciate. The slanted angle of the vase is carried through the main lines of the arrangement. If the left-side castor stem were not bent to create the pocket of space, this work would be ordinary. However, that single created angled line makes the loosely hanging lines of *Miscanthus* leaves and the space hold together.

Left: **Freestyle: Yellow patrinia.** Vase: Contemporary ceramic. Yellow patrinia was introduced earlier (see "The Seika Style" in Part II), as one of the seven autumnal herbs that have been well-known through the ages in Japan as *aki no nana gusa*. The seven are as follows: bush clover, *Miscanthus* grass, *kudzu* (kudzu is equivalent to *Pueraria lobata*), fringed pinks (*Dianthus superbus*), yellow patrinia, balloon flower (Chinese bell flower), and a chrysanthemum species. In this composition, the leaves of the *Miscanthus* stems have been stripped off so that the focus would be on the line quality of the plumes and stems. The irregular and delicately curling branches of yellow patrinia, which overlap the *Miscanthus* stems, provide accent to the total composition. This arrangement exudes the serene atmosphere of early evening in late summer.

Right: **Freestyle: Yellow patrinia.** Vase: Contemporary ceramic in a sharply pointed oval shape. The stems of yellow patrinia and *Miscanthus* grass are straight and difficult to bend, so generally they are left upright in line composition. In this arrangement, the leaves of both materials have been removed so that the straight lines become a main focus. However, in this creative composition, the yellow patrinia flower is arranged centrally in a careful line from the bottom to the top. A stem of wild poke with red leaves angles through the yellow patrinia column in a bold red line that is key to the design. The horizontally angled pink stems with berries add a sense of movement to the arrangement. Please notice that the *Miscanthus* plumes that blend with the yellow patrinia are mainly on the right-hand side. Active empty space is created on the left-hand side by the horizontally extended pink line in the lower part and the sparseness of the yellow blossoms at the top.

Left: **Freestyle: *Miscanthus* grass.** Vase: Contemporary clear glass bowl. In a clear glass bowl, this variegated *Miscanthus* grass is formed into various sizes of loops that are angled to make a nest. On a tabletop, this arrangement is reminiscent of a splash of water creating a green whirlpool that continues to spread out in different directions. Overripe Japanese cucumbers are placed in the center to hold the leaves in place. In contemporary flower arrangements, depending upon the creator's point of view, the line materials can be formed into mass or plane by rolling them up. So if the arranger has "plane" materials and wishes to create either lines or mass, first the side to use must be determined, and then the lines or mass can be formed. These creative adjustments in the materials are what make Ikebana both exciting and enjoyable for contemporary practitioners.

Freestyle: Yellow patrinia. Vase: Contemporary porcelain *suiban*. In this composition, the arranger has eliminated the straight stems and has given greater focus to the blossoms, with their finely divided branches. The artist has created a silver cylinder with a back rim to hold water and flowers in the ceramic vase. Yellow patrinia stems pierce the tube, and both ends of the tube have flowers in greater mass. The composition is housed in a contemporary flat dish-type container. The delicate texture of the patrinia varies from deep yellow to green, and with the visible line composition at the base of the flowers, this small but original design has its own beautiful charm.

Freestyle: Yellow patrinia. Vase: Contemporary ceramic. This novel design in a contemporary flower vase with an unusual outline promotes the artist's creative imagination. The lines of a species of rush have been carefully shaped and curved to complement the form of the flower vase. Yellow patrinia in the center serves as a focal point and complements the similar texture of the fruiting bodies of the rush, which are formed in a fan shape. The plant materials echo the outline of the flower vase. In this type of arrangement, the line quality of the individual stems is an important focus. There is a similarity to the work of the modern French painter Piet Mondrian, who focused on geometry and gridlike divisions of space. Notice the similar approach in the central part of this work: the crossing lines of the stems divide space into geometric patterns.

Freestyle: Yellow patrinia. Vase: Two identical contemporary flower vases of Hagiware. This beautiful composition of yellow patrinia and foxtail is reminiscent of a well-known early-seventeenth-century Japanese gold folding screen, decorated with a scene of autumnal grasses. The plant material is primarily crisscrossed in angles to give a sense of the density of an autumnal meadow. The foxtails, with their heads bending down, also suggest the richness of the autumn harvest. Hagiware is a special type of ceramic that comes only from Hagi kilns in Yamaguchi Prefecture in southern Japan.

A contemporary sculptural piece shown at the Ryusei annual exhibition. Large branches without leaves are used for this composition. Bittersweet berries are used as accent. The left-hand unit is larger than the right-hand side, but combined, they complete the work. Please notice that the cut surfaces of the branches are left in their natural white color to give additional accent.

A contemporary sculptural piece shown at the Ryusei annual exhibition. The oval form of this suspended work is created with wooden chopsticks that have been joined and then formed in layers, from large to small, to create a wreathlike structure. New Zealand flax leaves have been twisted around juniper branches and touch the floor, giving the illusion of a structure standing on its "toes."

SCULPTURAL PIECES

When the new movement in Ikebana—the free and abstract styles—emerged, they were called *objets d'art* in French. As is common practice in Japan, whenever a foreign term is introduced and is difficult to pronounce, it is "Japanized." That term today is *obuje* in Japan.

Freestyle covers a wide range in the naturalistic style. It doesn't consider shin, soe, or tai, but it still creates a "sketch of nature" representing a season. The abstract style no longer considers natural laws in the use of branches as lines, flat leaves as planes, and flowers as colorful mass. In abstract Ikebana, a tree can be upside down, petals can be used without the stem, and one type of material may be fastened to another with a straight pin. Petals may be used for color, size, and shape, more like paint from a palette. Such uses, all part of the new movement, would have been unthinkable in traditional Ikebana.

The abstract movement began in the nineteen fifties and sixties in Japan, and some Ikebana enthusiasts may remember exhibition pieces created solely in metal or in wood covered entirely with copper sheets. These creative pieces led to a reexamination of abstract Ikebana, though eventually this vogue faded away. As Grandmaster Kasen Yoshimura explains, the newest version of abstract Ikebana maintains that whatever the style or category, the core of the work must be constructed with materials that come from a plant. The main materials must not be metal or plastic. This influence is now the basis for works of contemporary Ikebana.

The contemporary arrangements on this page and the five pages that follow were created between 2001 and 2006 for the Ryusei Annual Exhibitions in Tokyo. These arrangements are selected and judged for both their beauty and uniqueness.

Above: **A contemporary sculptural piece shown at the Ryusei annual exhibition.** Dried sugar cane stalks were used to create this structure of circular forms both large and small. The forms were put together in such a way that the entire piece looks as if it has been suspended from above or is trying to grow outward. This is a unique contemporary composition. When Ikebana artists take part in large-scale Ikebana exhibitions, each artist is directed to the space provided. After sizing up the space, the artist creates a work to fit the space. Since these exhibitions last at least two weeks, the materials must be selected carefully so that there is no need to replace flowers or other materials.

Opposite: **A contemporary sculptural piece shown at the Ryusei annual exhibition.** This exhibition piece of contemporary Ikebana is unique in concept and form. The conelike structures, which suggest large sprouts growing out of the ground, are made of older branches, while younger branches of the same tree are woven through the cones to hold them in place. To the left, attached to the white column, is another unusual creation: strips of wood have been bent into unusual shapes, then some strips have been painted red and combined with the natural-colored strips.

Left: A contemporary sculptural piece shown at the Ryusei annual exhibition. Firewood is one of the favorite materials of this Ikebana artist. He has taken roots from vegetables such as ginger and a potato species and blended them with firewood to compose a pyramid structure. The texture and color gradients differ from those of flowers and branches, and the total effect creates quite a dynamic appearance. Split wood in combination with roots must be the artistic statement. How do you read it? Note the surrounding large works in the exhibition.

Right: A contemporary sculptural piece shown at the Ryusei annual exhibition. This type of work, like the previous two, is considered as installation Ikebana. Branches without leaves are composed like nerve fibers or tree roots extending into the soil. This work is accented with anthuriums in a variety of colors and with long green stems of asparagus ferns. Glass fishing-net floats serve as flower vases and are placed at various points to reflect light—giving an almost surreal feeling to the work.

Right: A contemporary sculptural piece shown at the Ryusei annual exhibition. This piece consists of a large juniper trunk, with some of its limbs attached and some detached branches bound with plastic tape to face toward each other. The photograph shows how a range of works is displayed at large-scale Ikebana exhibitions. Immediately to the left of the white column is an arrangement of dried lotus leaves suspended upside down, on many different levels, from the bare branches of a tree.

Above: **Contemporary Tai Saku.** The white boards are arranged in a dramatic formation. Like branches, the wood boards are a natural material, but they have been shaped by human hands. The arrangement is accented with purple orchids, small yellow orchids, baby's breath, palm leaves, and weeping mulberry branches, to create curved lines in contrast to the boards. This unique contemporary sculpturelike creation measures ten by twenty feet (height by width).

Opposite: **Contemporary installation of Ikebana.** In this contemporary Japanese interior design, there is a traditional *tokonoma* and a window, as is traditional for a tea ceremony room. However, the ceiling has a totally contemporary treatment and is covered with finely sliced strands of bamboo, woven like a mat. This Ikebana artist has met the challenge of the space by providing a complementary texture. Various types of bare vine branches begin at the center of the ceiling, wind down to the floor, then creep across the floor to the *tokonoma*, where they climb up the *tokonoma* wall, back to the ceiling. Dried materials are interwoven into the vine. This tea room is located in the Shimakin Restaurant in Kagurazaka, Tokyo.

Contemporary Tai Saku. This contemporary, fantasy filled installation is a masterwork of three-dimensionaility. Basketlike forms of woven bamboo—both horizontal and vertical—are supported by cylindrical metal flower containers suspended in the air. The flowers penetrate the woven bamboo, and many different types of flowers, vines, and branches are used to create a dreamlike or stage-set display. Combined with theatrical lighting and piped music, this dramatic display reveals a new dynamic direction in Ikebana art for the future.

PART III

Basic Tools and Techniques

Tools for Ikebana

As the techniques for arranging flowers continue to become more sophisticated, tools are redesigned to meet the needs. However, the basic tools—such as a small saw to cut thick branches, a hatchet to shave and shape thick branches, and scissors of various kinds, as developed by each Ikebana school—continue to be necessary. Today, a variety of equipment, much of it consisting of common garden tools, is being used as substitutes for the original basic tools.

The reader may substitute or improvise but must be aware that, although ordinary kitchen scissors or scissors designed to cut paper or cloth can be used to cut the thin stems of some flowers or to reshape a large leaf, they will not be strong enough to cut larger branches. Using them for that may result in damage to the scissors—or the user.

Various methods have been developed to make floral materials stand upright, or to shape or bend them into a desired angle. The thin wires used to support and shape floral materials have been around for some time, but vinyl and florist's tape are contemporary innovations. Although the kenzan has been in use since the beginning of the last century, modern innovations have made it easier to use, for all levels of Ikebana arrangers—professionals, amateurs, and beginners. The tools included in this book are primarily basic and traditional, but new innovations are constantly appearing on the market. *Note:* The "oasis" that Western florists use is not recommended for Ikebana because the foam will hold the materials, but it does not allow the angles of the plants to be readjusted.

Tips for finding basic Ikebana tools and supplies can be found in the Resource Guide at the end of this book.

BASIC TOOLS FOR ARRANGING FLOWERS

There are many useful tools available to help you manipulate floral matierals to acheive a desired form and to stabilize floral materials, including balancing top-heavy floral materials. The tools illustrated here are some of the most basic ones. Many of these tools are especially designed for flower arranging. Floral scissors, for example, are designed to cut through thick branches and differ greatly from scissors used to cut paper or cloth. All metal tools should be dried soon after use.

An assortment of flower holders and equipment. Beginning at the top and going clockwise: 1. A traditional flower holder; 2. A thin, textured black rubber disk, used to keep the *kenzan* from sliding; 3. Four small *kenzan*; 4. A *kenzan* needle repair tool; 5. A full-moon and half-moon *kenzan*, which can be interlocked as a unit; 6. A common oblong *kenzan*; 7. An oblong *kenzan* mat; 8. A *kenzan* with plastic needles.

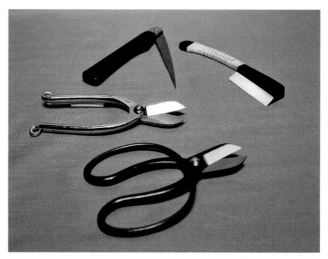

Various types of cutting tools. From top left going clockwise: 1. A folding V-shaped saw; 2. A small hatchet knife; 3. Large hoop-handled scissors; 4. Classic steel scissors. Please note that the blades of any of these scissors are sharp enough to shave branches.

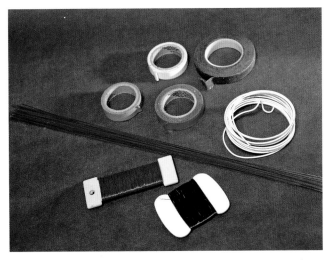

Various types of tapes and wires. The green, white, and blue tapes are common vinyl tapes. The large roll of green tape is florist's paper tape. It has an expandable crepe texture and is coated with heavy "sticky wax." The wires are common florist's wires. The thin black wire is the wire most popular with Ikebana practitioners. Thin, strong wire of this type is less visible than others and can be cut easily with flower scissors, without damaging the blades.

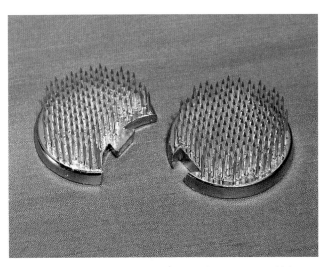

A popular full- and half-moon *kenzan* unit. Most *kenzan* are cast with brass needles in a lead base, for weight. It is important to wash and rinse *kenzan* well after each use to keep them in good condition.

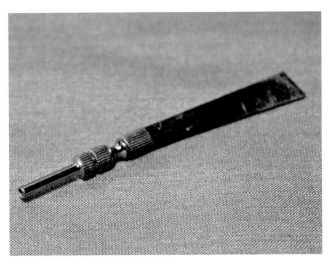

The thin brass needles of the *kenzan* often become bent as branches are penetrated and then forcibly angled. The repair tool has a hole in the bottom that allows it to slide over the bent needle and straighten it out. The blade end of the tool can be used to remove any floral materials remaining in the *kenzan*.

A traditional flower-stem holder made of lead (shown at the top), with a contemporary *kenzan* like device. The flower holder is placed on the device for ease of use. The lead flower holder was the type of apparatus used to hold flowers upright prior to the development of the *kenzan*. Today lead flower holders are used only by certain schools, for Seika arrangements.

A plastic *kenzan*. We are living in an age of plastics, so it follows that *kenzan* manufacturers have also utilized plastics. This *kenzan* with plastic needles—embedded in a lead base, for weight—is very useful for table centerpieces because under water the *kenzan* becomes almost invisible.

In a crystal bowl filled with water, the plastic "flower" becomes almost invisible. This plastic flower functions as a holder for floral materials in place of a common *kenzan* or the thick lead cablelike holder shown above.

Basic Ikebana Techniques

Ikebana can be translated as "living flowers" and, as with all living things, each type of plant has its own set of characteristics. While handling a wide spectrum of plants, an Ikebana artist develops an all-important working knowledge of the characteristics of different plants.

In this process of trial and error, the artist learns to apply different techniques to different plant materials. For our purposes in arranging flowers, the word "characteristic" is broad and all-encompassing. However, the major characteristic that we concern ourselves with is whether a plant's stem or branch is brittle or supple. The two major groups are:

- Plants with very brittle stems and branches that require special treatment. Even minute attempts at bending will cause them to break.
- Plants with supple branches that can be successfully bent into the desired shape or angle with the use of proper techniques.

Various techniques are used to shape and bend individual plant materials to obtain the desired curvature. This chapter will show you the fundamental techniques that an Ikebana arranger uses when handling the various types of plant materials.

METHODS FOR HANDLING BRANCHES

When arranging branches, in most cases, you are faced with the task of bending the branch to the desired shape and removing the unnecessary lesser branches. The degree and angle of bending will vary according to your needs. The photograph at the top (left) of page 141 shows the technique of using both hands to create a gentle bend. You can also use heat to create a gentle bend.

Seika: Right-hand pattern. In this arrangement soe has its own natural curve and is farily flexible. To help augment or maintain this natural curve, heat may be utilized, as illustrated on the opposite page. Always remember to hide burn marks from the viewer's sight.

USING HEAT

You may also use heat to create a bend, as some branches may be easier to bend this way than others. Whether or not to use this technique is a matter of personal preference. Before heating the branch fill a container with cold water. Choose a container large and deep enough for the section of the heated branch to be immersed in water.

Most branches can be bent with both hands. It is important to give strong support to both the bottom and top of the branch with the palm and fingers of your left hand, while you gently begin bending with your right hand.

A successful bend, shown here, requires patience. Treat the branch as an extension of yourself, and feel the branch's movements and tendencies. You must "talk to it" to successfully bend it.

Using heat to create a bend. Many types of evergreen have heavy sap, which can be useful when using the heating technique. Sap becomes soft when heated and becomes hard again when cooled.

During this process, you will hear a crackling sound. Place the part of the branch you wish to bend over the candle flame, all the while gently bending it into the desired angle.

When the desired angle has been achieved, immediately plunge the heated section into cold water. Hold it there until it is completely cool.

The new angle is now stabilized. If required, or if you wish, paint the burnt section with a color that matches the original bark.

CREATING A SHARPLY BENT ANGLE

In arrangements such as Nageire sharply bent angles may be necessary to anchor floral materials and to keep them at a certain angle above the rim of the vase.

As shown in the photograph on page 141 (top left), when bending for a curvature your palm should be used as a supporting cushion. However, bending at a sharp angle means that you will give the branch a gentle break. Therefore, as shown here, give support with your fingers as you gently but forcibly create a small break in the branch.

This shows a successful bend at a sharp angle. Although the upper part is broken, the lower bark is still intact, and water can still be transported to the leaves and upper branches. If the break is too severe and will not hold the desired angle, make a half-splint and wire it on. (See page 149 for instructions on how to wire floral materials.)

Before you proceed with the branch you plan to bend, try a sample branch to test the nature or character of the material. Maples and some varieties of oak are brittle and have a tendency to snap and break when you forcibly bend them, so they are not suitable for this technique.

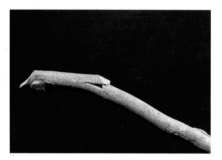

To create a bend, make a cut at an angle that is one-half the diameter of the branch.

Gently open the break so that the upper bark overlaps.

Using this method, you can give curvature to the branch.

Using Scissors. Some stems and branches cannot be sharply bent because of the nature of the plant material. Some branches—such as maple or flowering plum—will simply break in two. For these materials, you must use scissors to create a bend. In this technique, several shallow cuts are made that allow brittle branches to be gently and gradually bent. If the sharply bent angle will be in clear view, you can use the wedge technique, which will be more aesthetically pleasing. In the wedge technique, one deep cut is made, so this technique is not recommended for brittle branches.

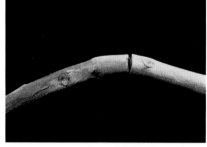

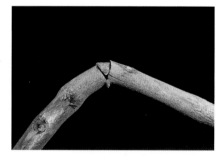

To use the wedge technique, make a cut at an angle that is perpendicular to the branch. How deep you cut will depend on the thickness of the branch as well as the weight of the leaves the branch must support.

Gently bend to open the cut in the branch. If you bend the branch too rapidly, it will break in half.

Use the same branch material to cut a small wedge and insert. The tendency of the branch is to spring back, so the wedge will be held in place.

HOW TO SHAPE LEAVES AND STEMS

Advanced Ikebana requires that the floral materials be adjusted to fit a design. This sometimes means that a leaf or stem must be reshaped. Sometimes specific adjustments must be made to overcome the natural tendencies of the plant materials.

Most plant leaves can be shaped gently. This aspidistra has natural curves in its leaves, but the center rib is very straight.

The aspidistra can be bent as shown here because it is a fairly flexible leaf. It can be rolled in a tubular form to achieve a similar effect.

This and the next two photographs illustrate the fundamental method of giving curvature to a leaf. This shaping technique will not work on leaves without a strong center vein.

Front view, using the same technique. You must stretch the leaf and apply pressure from underneath simultaneously. When working with iris, and many other leaves that have a center rib vein, place your fingers underneath where you wish to form a bend or curve.

Some leaves can be curved quite easily because the top surface will stretch, in much the same way the smooth side of soft tanned leather will stretch. Be careful with certain types of leaves, such as iris, that have a powdery white surface. If you rub and vigorously stretch these types of leaves, the places you touch will become artificially shiny. *Caution:* Certain types of leaves, such as pampas grass, have fine sawtooth edges. For these, the sliding movement for bending is from the base to the tip. If you reverse the movement, you can cut your fingers.

Tulips and Dutch irises are among the plants whose inner stem is very soft and holds a great deal of liquid. This stem can also be made straight or bent. The plant in this example is a calla lily.

To form a curvature, place your fingers underneath the stem and gently press toward the desired direction. If you try to bend without the support of your fingers, you will break the stem. (The xylem and phloem tubes, which transport water and food for the plant, will break at that point.)

Another technique is to support the stem by holding it in the palm of your hand and gently pulling down, as if you're stretching the stem. As the left palm goes up, the right hand pulls down.

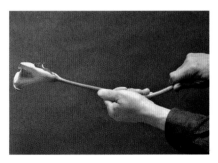

Another method is to hold the stem in your palm and fingers, as in the previous example, and apply a gentle pressure down toward your palm, while the right hand pulls the stem toward you.

HOW TO USE WIRE SUPPORTS

Hollow-stemmed flowers can be easily straightened with thin wire, as illustrated here.

The gerbera often comes with a plastic protective cup on the blossom, and it is placed in a box with the flower facing up, when it is shipped from the farm to market. A flower such as the gerbera will often have a bent stem near the blossom.

As shown in this example, it can be straightened out quite easily. Fortunately, the gerbera has a hollow stem, so one can insert a straight wire for support. If you wish to have a special curvature, that is also very easy to do.

A green vinyl tape is used at the bottom of the stem to keep it from splitting. (For information about securing the stems, see pages 147–49.) Close to the blossom, the neck of the stem is not hollow, so support the neck with your fingers and gently push the wire through to the base of the blossom.

HOW TO SHAPE FLOWER PETALS

With patience and a gentle touch, nearly all parts of floral materials can be coerced to take new shapes. Flower petals are no exception.

Most blossoms with large petals, especially those with thick petals—such as tulips—can be persuaded to open up, even if the flower is originally tight.

First gently open and stretch the petal, then rub the surface lightly to turn it back

Every other petal has been opened. Notice how the visual effect is totally different.

All six petals have been opened up and flipped backward, to create a completely different look. This technique can be applied to many other flowers.

HOW TO SHAPE LARGE LEAVES

Large leaves add drama to arrangements, and are simple to shape and stabilize, as demonstred in these four photographs.

A large leaf has been inserted at its base.

To reduce the size, cut the leaf to the desired shape.

This technique can be applied to any large flat leaf.

Here the leaf has been cut to the desired shape.

HOW TO USE THE KENZAN TO HOLD FLORAL MATERIALS

The kenzan is the most popular and useful tool for stabilizing floral materials, both large and small. Kenzan come in a variety of sizes and shapes, and an arranger must decide which is the most appropriate. All tools, large or small, have limitations, and this should be taken into consideration no matter what is it that you wish to accomplish.

Most branches have solid, hard stalks that are difficult to push onto the *kenzan* needles. The photographs here demonstrate some common techniques for using a *kenzan* with stalks of this nature.

Most branch stalks can be cut at an angle to facilitate insertion in a *kenzan*. Center your body weight directly above—and not at an angle—or you can injure your fingers.

Unlike loop-handled scissors, these scissors allow you to apply your body weight on the scissors to cut through the stalk. To avoid crushing your fingers, make sure the small loop at the end of the scissors is in contact with the table.

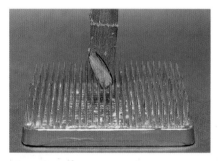

Cutting the stalk at this angle makes it easier to insert and stabilize the branch. This is a good method for an upright position.

Cut both sides to make a sharp edge, then insert.

For thicker branch stalks, like the one shown here, cut a portion away to make the bottom of the branch thinner. Use both hands to push the branch forcibly onto the *kenzan* needles.

An additional technique that makes it easier to insert a branch into the *kenzan* is to split it with crosscuts several times.

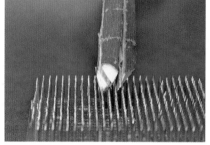

First slide the branch stalk in upright. Crosscut splitting is a useful technique for any branch stalk.

Maintain continuous pressure downward as you push the stalk in at the desired angle.

HOW TO STABILIZE SPLITTING STEMS

A kenzan is an effective tool for Ikebana. However, the sharp nails that hold floral materials in place can sometimes cause damage to the cut surface of the stem, when force is used to push it in place. The following illustrated techniques will help you avoid damaging your floral materials.

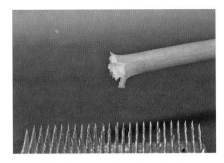

Plants with soft stems, such as the calla lily, naturally develop multidirectional splits that curl up when the stem is put in a *kenzan*.

To prevent the natural tendency of soft stems to split and curl up, wrap the bottom of the stem with vinyl tape.

If the floral material is to be placed at an angle, splint a thin, hard stalk to the main stem. This will help keep the stem rigid.

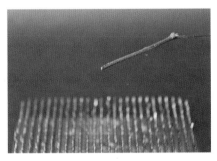

If you are using thin-stemmed material such as baby's breath or *Limonia*—also called "misty"—wire a supporting splint to it, to make the base thicker. (For detailed instructions, see page 149.)

The thin stem with adequate support can now be placed in the *kenzan*. Cut both sides to make a sharp edge, then insert.

Small chrysanthemum stems and other fine-stemmed materials can be bundled and wired together to make one larger stem.

Once the stems are wired together, they can be inserted in the *kenzan*.

HOW TO STABILIZE HOLLOW STEMS

Kenzan needles will not satisfactorily support hollow-stemmed material. The technique illustrated here will allow you to use hollow-stemmed floral materials, such as gerbera, with a kenzan.

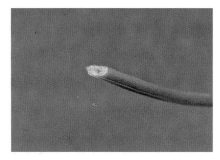

Floral materials that have hollow stems, such as gerbera, require added support for use in a *kenzan* (thin *kenzan* needles won't hold them).

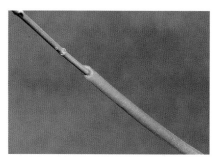

To allow the gerbera to be supported by the *kenzan*, insert a harder and slightly smaller stem into the gerbera's hollow stem. Before removing the smaller stem, cut it off at the bottom so that it is nearly flush with the bottom of the gerbera—leaving just enough stem so that you can extract it from the gerbera.

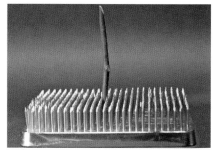

Place the support stem into the *kenzan* in the upright position first, for plant material such as a gerbera.

Move the stem to the desired angle.

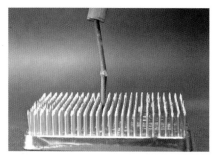

If your floral material has a curved stem, maintaining the angle will create greater stress, so it is best to use vinyl tape on the end.

Gently push the stem of the floral material onto the supporting stem, and you will have the desired angle.

HOW TO BALANCE HEAVY FLORAL MATERIALS

Certain floral materials, especially large branches with many leaves or needles, may be too top-heavy for the kenzan you are using.

A *kenzan* may not be able to support the weight of large branches with leaves.

Above: Place another *kenzan* upside down and use it as a stabilizing anchor.

Right: Now the large maple branch can stand at an angle. A counterbalancing *kenzan* like this may be needed in your arrangement, especially for a branch angled in this manner. Use other floral materials to camouflage the *kenzan*.

HOW TO USE THIN WIRE TO ATTACH A SUPPORT

Certain types of cut floral materials have very soft or thin stems. Placing such material in a kenzan without firm support can be difficult, whether it is to be upright or at an angle.

First cut the support splint to the desired length, then place it along the main stem. With your left hand, hold one end of the thin wire at the top of the splint. Gently but firmly pull the wire to the bottom of the splint and floral material.

Begin winding the wire, leaving space at the end of the stem (where you will later cut it and place it under water). Wind in a spiral, coming toward you as you go, all the while keeping the wire taut. With each turn of the wire, move your thumb up to hold the last spiral, until you reach the top of the splint.

When you reach the desired length, usually an inch or two, wrap the wire around several times at the top to secure the proper tension.

While using your left thumb to hold the coiled wire taut and secure, pull out the other end with your right hand.

Hold the two ends in your right hand and, in a circular motion, twist the wire between your finger and thumb to form a short coil. Keep twisting until the ends are tight at the base.

Cut the wires to about $1^{1}/_{2}$ inches from the stem to the tip of the wire. Then cut about $^{1}/_{8}$ inch off the end of the stem under water to refresh it.

Bend the cut ends over to make a loop, and then twist it to make it secure.

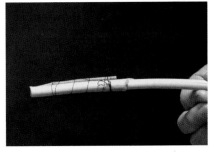

Push the loop down and press it against the surface of the stem. The loop is for safety—when wires are left sticking out, they can pierce your fingers quite easily.

Now the supporting splint will help to secure the stem in the *kenzan*. The examples in these photos have not been cut and placed in water, but for a real arrangement, always leave a portion of the lower stem without wires so that the end can be cut under water.

MAINTAINING FRESHNESS IN FLORAL MATERIALS

Plants naturally obtain water from the ground, but when floral materials are cut for making an arrangement, the long tubes that carry water from root to stem have been cut. The arranger must provide a simulated method for the cut floral materials to get water. Air bubbles and bacteria are the biggest problems to overcome. To prolong the life of flowers in a vase, change the water daily or every other day, and add a touch of salt, a drop of detergent, or "cut-flower food" from a florist.

Pond lilies pose a particular challenge because it is difficult to get them to draw water. To maintain freshness, I recommend dusting the stems in powdered alum, then placing them in water. For other kinds of water lilies, I recommend diluting about one teaspoon of either vinegar or salt in a gallon of water. Then pump the solution directly into the stem tubes with a syringelike tool.

The first step to reviving wilted leaves and flower petals is to trim the ends of the stems and soak them in water, as described in the caption below (left). If this does not work, give the stems a hot water treatment, as described in the caption below (right). If your flowers are still not revived, fill a bathtub with cold water and immerse them for a few hours.

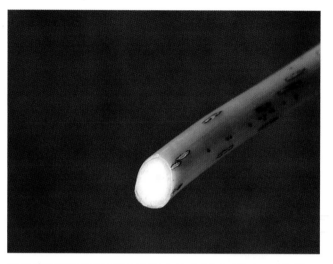

Water prolongs the life and beauty of floral material. Thus, you should always cut your floral materials with a few inches to spare, so that the final cut, after preparation, can be done under water. If the last cut is in the air, an air bubble will form and prevent water from moving up the xylem tubes that carry water up the stem of the plant.

Some plants have stems with a hard outer surface but an inner part that is soft and spongy, like cotton or Styrofoam. Roses, chrysanthemums, and hydrangeas fit this category and must be cut under water. Often, with this category of floral materials, you will get good results if, after cutting the stem under water, you immediately plunge it into boiling hot water for a few minutes, then again quickly immerse it in cold water. This boosts the moving of water upward in the xylem tubes. It also removes air bubbles and kills bacteria. Remember to wrap the upper stem and leaves with wet paper or cloth for protection from steam when plunging floral material in a hot bath. Only the stems should receive this treatment.

ARRANGEMENT IN THE KUBARI

In the history of Ikebana, erecting floral materials, such as branches, in a perpendicular form was revolutionary, especially in the sense that the inside of the vase was as important as what was seen above the vase. Equally important is that when the V-shaped kubari holds a branch, in Seika, parts such as soe and taisaki sweep out in angles toward the back or the front—yet, above the kubari, the stems must appear as a single unit, in a trunklike fashion. Therefore, in Seika, the underwater stems must be forcibly bent in the same direction as the part that is visible. This creates tension among the floral materials, pushing them together, and makes a tight bundle as the arrangement rises above the rim.

In Nageire, the bottom end of the floral materials—which is underwater—continues in the same direction as the upper part.

This diagram shows how above the rim of the vase the stems in a Seika arrangement must appear as one unit. The circles are cross-sections of the *kubari*.

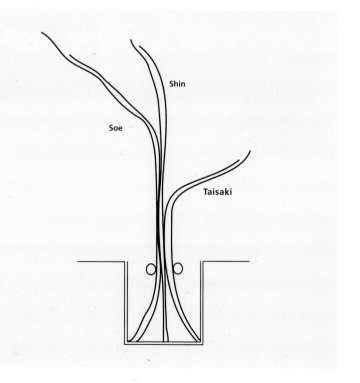

TRADITIONAL STABILIZING TECHNIQUES

When Ikebana was in its infancy, the kenzan and other modern materials used to stabilize floral materials were not available. Ikebana artist developed ingenious methods that are still useful for today's practitioners of Ikebana.

Using a V-shaped short branch with an additional crosspiece can be very useful to hold floral materials erect. A variety of containers can be used, from flat to tall, and in many diverse shapes. Vase materials can vary from cast bronze to bamboo. The container shown here is bronze, and the lower stand comes apart from the top part, which holds the water.

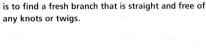

The first step when creating a Seika arrangement is to find a fresh branch that is straight and free of any knots or twigs.

Shave one end off each piece at an angle, so that they will fit together to make a V. Use a knife or flower scissors to make the contact surface smooth. Cut off all buds and small branch ends as close as possible to the main stalk, to make it smooth.

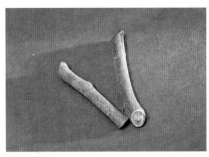

Select suitable parts of the branch and cut the pieces slightly longer than the diameter of the section that holds water. Heavier floral materials will require a branch piece that is thicker in diameter. Lightweight floral materials will require a thinner piece.

Wire the shaved sides together to make a V-shape. To keep it stabilized, secure it with wire in two places.

Place the V on the opening of the vase to measure the exact length. Make allowances for the slanted ends to extend beyond the diameter of the mouth of the vase. All three ends must be cut at a slant. These slanted ends are the part of the branch that will fit snugly when the V is pressed into the mouth of the vase, and that will provide firm support. (For a more detailed view of ends cut at a slant, see the photograph on page 153.)

Forcibly push the V down so that it is firmly in place, about ¹/₂-inch from the rim of the vase. If you can pick up the vase with the V-shaped insert in place, then it is pressed in firmly enough.

Based upon the type of materials you plan to use for your Seika arrangement, the V-shape shown to the left, inserted in the container, may be too narrow to hold the floral materials in place. The natural V-shape, shown in the far right of this photograph, is cut from a branch with a much wider opening, which is suitable for thick stalks such as evergreens. Depending on the materials you plan to use, you may wish to select a suitable naturally formed V-shape.

Now make the third crosspiece. The third piece must be cut longer than necessary, then cut and shaped so it will stay firmly in place when inserted to hold the plant materials After the first two branches of shin and soe have their length and curvature determined, they will be held upright with this crosspiece. Then they will be removed, and the other seven to nine floral materials will be cut, shaped, and added: beginning with taisaki, which will fit into the point of the V in the very front. When all the necessary parts for the arrangement are inserted into the V-shape, readjust the length of the crosspiece. Then forcibly push it in and firmly press it against the arrangement to hold it in place.

TECHNIQUES FOR THE NAGEIRE STYLE

In the Nageire style, the floral material leans against the mouth of a flower vase. The following photos will show some common practices for obtaining the required angles and spacing.

Here a single short branch fits the diameter of the container.

This shows the technique of using two short branch pieces that fit snugly in the vase, making a perpendicular cross.

Use a Y-shaped branch piece fitted snugly, as is used in Seika.

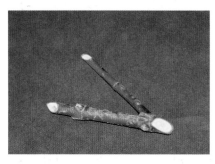

The ends of any support branch should be cut at a slight angle and slightly longer than the actual diameter, so that the branch can be placed firmly in the vase. This gives it strength, but enough give to support the weight of materials without breaking.

A cross-stalk is another technique to stabilize materials. As shown here, a piece of twig is wired directly onto floral material. The stalk must be cut to the size of the diameter of the vase. For safety, loop the end of the wire. (For instructions on how to wire plant material, see page 149.)

Plant material with a supporting cross-stalk. Please note that the stalk must fit the diameter firmly to hold the stem in place.

Far left: Using a supporting cross-stalk, this comparatively large plant material is securely braced without touching the bottom of the vase.

Left: Floral materials generally grow according to their own curvature; therefore, when you place them in a vase they may flip over, to face in the other direction, simply because of gravitational force.

To create the angle you want, break the stem so that the floral material will face in the desired direction. (*Note:* This is a partial break, made by bending the interior water-carrying tubes at a sharp angle, but not severing them.) The break is made so that the stem will brace itself against the inner wall of the container.

Close-up view of the technique.

The natural curvature of the stem of this calla lily makes the flower face down.

Bending the stem in the other direction will make it press against the container wall, to face at the desired direction and angle. The length of the section of stem below the break determines the angle of the stem.

This calla lily is veering to the right. If you wish floral material to stand upright, the following is a simple technique.

The bottom of the stem is sharply bent up, utilizing the natural springlike tendency of the plant to hold it erect.

If your floral material is light in weight, the simplest technique for maintaining the desired angle is to cut the stem at an angle.

Close-up view of the cut stem.

Left: A heavy lead "wire" is twisted and placed in the vase to help stabilize floral materials at various angles. The heavy lead does give weight to the vase, but if you are using a glass or crystal vase you might wish to use less obvious materials, such as copper or bronze wire or a crumpled mesh of chicken wire.

Right: Heavy lead wire is used to keep a tulip securely positioned.

CONTEMPORARY RIKKA ARRANGEMENTS

The twenty-first century continues to be increasingly fast-paced, and this affects the creative processes in art as well. When Rikka was developed, practitioners had the great luxury of time. All of the classic arts, be it oil painting or sculpting in marble, accumulated their techniques and wisdom from a time when life was slower-paced. Some of that wisdom can be applied to the arts today, which is the strength of classic training in the arts.

These twisted branches are in the style of the Sunamono category of Rikka. The uniquely shaped branches are formed by assembling various sized parts, the smaller of which are numbered to facilitate reassembly. Nail points protruding from the small branches will hold pine needles that have been reassembled with wire and slid onto the nails to give a lifelike effect. Pieces of rice straw, about four or five inches in length, will be made into bundles, joined together in a chainlike fashion, circled around the lower main trunk, and secured with a hemp cord. This tight rim around the base of the main trunk will form a foundation that functions both as a stabilizing force and as a *kenzan* to hold other plant materials. The whole unit will be immersed in a square or oblong shallow basin. River-polished pebbles will cover the square board that stabilizes the main trunk.

The tree branches that have been assembled and attached to the main stem are the *shin*, or main, *soe*, or secondary, and *nagashi*, or tertiary branches. For the completed arrangement, see page 54 in the Sunamono discussion of Rikka (Part II). *Note:* In Japan, rice straw is readily available, but in the United States this is not the case, so any tubular shape, such as plastic roll-up shades, can be used, to improvise. The plastic material should be hollow on the inside, such as "drinking straws," so that you can bundle them and use them as supports, just as you would natural rice straw. Also, plastic will not deteriorate like rice straw. In the photograph opposite plastic "straw" is used. This technique can be used to stabilize any large structure or "trunk" in an arrangement.

Close-up view of main trunk, showing where the two pieces of the main shin branch will interlock. (Information concerning the connecting point is written on the crosscut piece with *sumi* ink.)

Small pieces of bamboo are shaped in a special way and nailed onto one of the adjoining pieces. A slot is carved into the other piece so that the two pieces will interlock.

A detail of the plastic "straws," as seen from above.

Originally, rice straw was used in large Rikka arrangements before the invention of the *kenzan* to stabilize the arrangement and hold additional material. Here plastic "straws" were used. In this arrangement the attached *do*, or main body part, is covered with an aspidistra leaf. The green cups will hold water for flowers and can be easily attached.

MID- TO LARGE-SCALE CONTEMPORARY ARRANGEMENTS

Ikebana arrangers of mid- to large-scale works may employ modern electric tools to achieve their goals. As the next sequence of photographs illustrates, materials provided by nature can be rearranged and enhanced with the use of the electric drill.

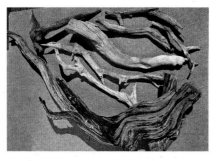

The artist gathered weathered wood to use for the arrangement on the opposite page. When working with weathered wood, you will often find that some parts are very hard, and some very soft, light, and crumbly. This will depend on how much sap is present (sap acts as a preservative). Generally, heavier material will have more sap in it; however, some woods, such as ebony, are naturally heavy.

Plan your composition first, then use a drill to assemble the materials. First drill a hole that extends through both the top and bottom pieces.

Next, join the pieces with a screw. Make sure that the screw is long enough to secure them strongly together.

This photograph shows the two pieces joined, with the screw head visible.

If you wish to hide the screw head, or if you don't have a screw long enough to hold the two pieces together, use a larger bit to drill a larger hole, partway down.

The screw now goes through the wider opening, down into the wood.

The screw is now deep in the wood. Use a long screw-head bit in the drill, so it will reach the screw in the hole.

The screw joining the two pieces is now in place, deep in the hole. Generally, in large-scale arrangements, these holes are not highly noticeable. However, when you feel it is necessary to hide the hole completely, fill it in with a matching color of carpenter's crayon.

A supporting and balancing board has been added. It is inserted in the vase and is therefore invisible to viewers. Measure the height and the mouth of the vase to determine the width and length of the support. To adequately secure this board for support, four screws were used.

Opposite: **Freestyle.** Vase: Large ceramic. The artist who created this contemporary arrangement, which was completed for an outdoor courtyard, incorporated stargazer lilies and the driftwood shown above, and the techniques illustrated above. Its measurements are five feet in height and six feet in width. The vase is 32 inches high, with a mouth 16 inches wide. The stand is 25 inches tall. James Wayne, a retired ceramics instructor from San José City College, created the vase.

Lessons in Ikebana

Lessons in Seika

All art forms strive to bring pleasure and a viewer who is deeply moved experiences a desire to create that art. When beautiful art at its highest level is observed, this is a common reaction. Flower arrangements are created from materials that surround us daily. Inspired by the beauty of nature, anyone can pick up a pair of scissors and begin to arrange flowers.

But if one has knowledge of some of the basic rules and concepts, tested and developed by generations of Ikebana masters, then one's approach to making an arrangement is more likely to be successful. Certainly, one can spend a lifetime mastering an art form. The basic lessons in Part IV will start you on that path.

In the study or practice of Seika, it is important to become familiar with the individual components and their formations in lines. To learn this, pussy willows are ideal because they are easy to bend and shape. The side that is generally exposed to the sun (*yang*) is colorful, and the side that is mainly in shade (*yin*) is basically green.

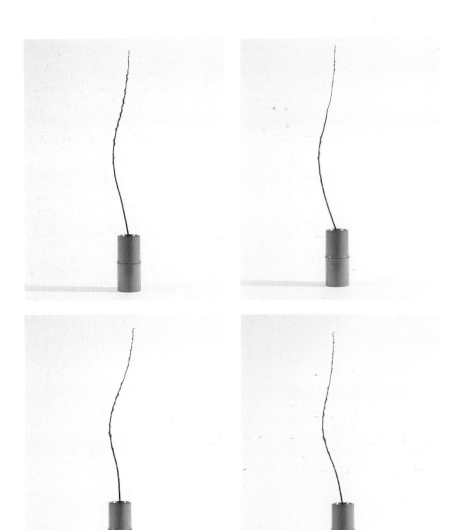

Far left: **This photograph shows the upper part of the shin curvature in standard formation. However, when one uses line materials such as pussy willows, it is important to give the feeling of the energy or strength of the plant growth, so toward the tip, it becomes almost straight. The lower part is slightly angled to the left, instead of being perpendicular to the rim of the vase. It is important that an imaginary straight line from the tip of shin to the very bottom be perpendicular to the rim of the vase.**

Left: **This example shows that the line is perpendicular, but the lower part is not properly curved, and it veers off to the left too quickly.**

Far left: **Overall curvature in this example is close to being correct, but it needs to lean slightly to the left. The curvature is also too tight, and the imaginary line veers way off to the right.**

Left: **In this example the perpendicular line veers to the left.**

Seika: Nishu Ike in informal pattern. Vase: Cast bronze with a dragon motif. This Seika arrangement of redbud branches and yellow chrysanthemums has a lower point in the shin curvature than the Seika arrangement of pussy willows and white chrysanthemums shown on page 162. Because of the given curvature in shin, dynamic and curved branches were selected for the soe branch, which extend far to the left. To achieve balance, the taisaki chrysanthemums extend out to the right. The overall visual effect of the arrangement is wider to the left and right, giving it a more relaxed feeling than the formal arrangement of pussy willows.

Seika: Nishu Ike in informal pattern made with pussy willows and chrysanthemums. Vase: Bamboo. This arrangement is in the category of *Nishu Ike* (two different materials in a formal pattern). *Nishu Ike* is a popular choice when using seasonal branches for shin and soe, and seasonal flowers for *taisaki*. *Taisaki* flowers are placed in front of the branches. *Tai mikomi*, in this case flowers, should be pushed back to create a sense of depth, which is their function. There should be an obvious division of space between the *shin* and *soe* units: the individual branches should never be the same height, and lines should never crisscross. After completion, the arrangement should be given a spray of water. The bamboo vase is placed on a board, which is used to avoid staining a table-top or *tatami*, or simply as a matter of taste. The numbered list below corresponds with numbered positions in the arrangement and inset diagram.

1. Shin
2. The shin back complement follows shin up to the peak of the curvature on the left, then gradually separates off to the right.
3. The shin front complement follows shin up one-third of the way from the bottom, then remains to the left, with its tip going straight up. You have thus created an irregular or scalene triangle formation connecting the tips of these three branches.
4. Soe is placed in the kenzan next to the shin on the left-hand side. The soe line separates from the shin line at one-quarter the distance from the rim of the vase. Aim for the left back at less than 45 degrees.
5. Soe back complement will be placed behind soe and follow it, leaving space almost midpoint between shin and soe. It veers slightly toward the back of the soe line.
6. The front complement of soe follows soe and comes slightly forward.
7. The tai branch is placed right in front of the shin and soe unit. It should follow the shin line, but it will veer slightly left of the shin front accompaniment.
8. Additional accompaniments, when added, are placed between the tai and shin front complements and follow the shin curve line. The function is to fill space between shin and shin accompaniments.
9. White chrysanthemums or any other light-colored chrysanthemums of your choice can be used, but look for stems with good leaves. Chrysanthemum's number-9 position, taisaki, is supposed to be 60 percent the height of soe, but it has much greater mass than line materials, so it is placed lower at the center front of all the units and is angled to the right. Leave a space between taisaki and the pussy willow unit.
10. Chrysanthemum number 10 is *tani* and will be placed immediately behind taisaki. Among the three blossoms, it is the largest.
11. Chrysanthemum 11 is tai mikomi and will be placed almost next to the shin unit, between it and tai. It should lean to the back. Tai mikomi will be perpendicular or slightly to the right.

Step 1: For the beginner in Seika, using a *kenzan* will be easier, but one can also begin by using the V-shaped *kubari* in a traditional bamboo tube flower vase (shown above).

Step 2: Among the available branches of pussy willows, select the one that has the most dominating presence and has the thickness and height that is appropriate for *shin* (1). Then select both the *back* (2) and *front* (3) *complements* to complete the shin unit. These will be the tallest branches, but *soe* (4) is another important branch that requires thickness and is second only to shin. Complements for shin require height plus a certain character but are not necessarily as thick as shin. Then both the *front* (6) and *back* (5) *complements* for soe will be selected. *Tai* (7), which here literally means "body," is placed in front of the shin unit and thus should have a thicker stem than the complement branches.

Step 3: Select shin and soe, the two branch units, which are described below. After you've selected them, lay them down on the table in that order.

The shin group: Shin is tallest, the back complement slightly shorter, and the front complement is shorter than the back complement.

The soe group: Soe height should be 60 percent of shin after it has been bent and shaped. Therefore, it is always wise to cut it slightly longer.

Step 4: Shin will be bent in a bow shape, then placed in the center of the kubari or kenzan. (Please study the diagram on this page for the formation of the curvature and placement of the kubari.) Measuring from the rim of the vase to the tip of shin, the peak of the curvature is exactly at midpoint (see the bottom left diagram on page 62).

After you have selected the shin and have given it the proper curvature, place it in the kenzan or the kubari. Shin should be placed perpendicular to the kenzan in an imaginary straight line to the tip. Then put the *ki dome* in place to make the branch stand. (The ki dome is the piece that holds plant materials in the kubari. For constructing a kubari and ki dome see pages 150–51 in "Basic Ikebana Techniques," Part III.) Check the diagram on page 150, then select the next branches for the proper thickness and length for soe and tai. Hold soe behind the vase to see if it is suitable, then give it an initial curvature and cut. (*Note:* Always make sure you cut your materials longer than needed for the final arrangement.) Place it in the kubari directly behind shin, 45 degrees to the left and 45 to 50 degrees forward. Check the photograph and diagram on page 162, for the number and position. Next give the tai branch the same treatment for both size and curvature; then cut.

Now select your shin front and back complements. First, individually hold them outside and behind shin, to determine curvature and lengths. Place them in the kubari as shown in the diagram on page 162.

Proceed with complementary branches for both soe and tai. Hold each limb up and compare it with the main branch for curvature and length. Once all of the branches have been shaped and cut in proper lengths, place them in the vase, then remove them in reverse order, starting with the back, and place them on the table in that same order. When placing the materials in the final arrangement, you will begin from the front, putting the *tai* materials in first. Finally, you will place the ki dome in firmly to hold the arrangement in place.

SHIN CURVATURES

Branches may sometimes have natural curves and perhaps limbs that can serve as soe or the complementary lines of shin or soe. Therefore you can be flexible when making artistic judgments about angles and curves. A natural branch may appear to have a perfect main curvature, but perhaps in reality it is lower than the required standard. The diagram below (right) shows the standard peak curvature for shin. The diagram below (left) shows a peak curvature that is lower than the standard. In such cases, the height at which soe and taisaki branch off from shin is lower than the standard.

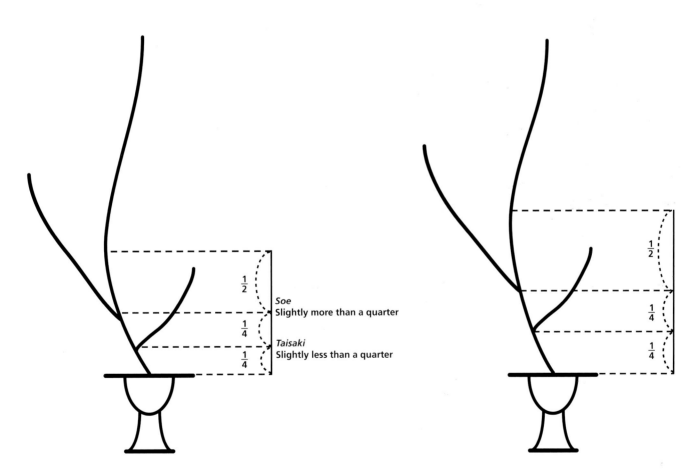

$\frac{1}{2}$

Soe
Slightly more than a quarter

$\frac{1}{4}$

Taisaki
Slightly less than a quarter

$\frac{1}{4}$

$\frac{1}{2}$

$\frac{1}{4}$

$\frac{1}{4}$

A diagram of a left-hand arrangement with lower-than-standard proportions for *soe* and *taisaki*. Here the apex of the *shin* branch is lower, requiring the *soe* and *taisaki* to be adjusted accordingly. This adjustment is made if your floral materials dictate that the widest point of the curvature of *shin* should be lower than the standard.

A diagram of a left-hand arrangement with standard proportions for *soe* and *taisaki*. In this diagram the apex of the curvature is at the midpoint of the total height of *shin*.

NINE LEAVES OF ASPIDISTRA

It has been said that lessons in Seika begin and end with aspidistra. In the previous lessons with pussy willows, it was necessary to learn the total formation as well as the proportions in height. With aspidistra, after you have become acquainted with the basics, the next step is to learn how the leaf surface can be divided into the yin and yang side. Aspidistra leaves are reasonably easy for beginners to handle. The example arrangement (below, left) is an Isshu Ike in an informal pattern. The vase is a bamboo tube style.

yang is the wider side

yin is the narrower side

Most plant leaves appear to be bilaterally symmetrical on either side of the main vein. Yet, upon close examination, often they are not all bilaterally symmetrical. If this is the case, the wider side is called yang and the narrow side is called *yin*. Using this distinction, the wider side of the leaf must be toward the front part of the arrangement, and the smaller side toward the back.

After you have finalized the selection of your nine leaves, according to the placement of the leaves, you might need to straighten a leaf or give curvature to it. If you need to straighten a leaf, roll the leaf and then gently stretch it by pulling up and down simultaneously, as show in the photograph above. If you wish to bend a leaf, roll the leaf from the tip downward.

The nine leaves of aspidistra are shown below. The numbers indicate their placement in the *kenzan* or *kubari*.
1. *Taisaki* (at the very front)
2. *Tani* (required to create effect of a worm-eaten leaf, to shorten it and to give it a different appearance from the others)
3. *Tai*
4. Front accompaniment of *shin*
5. *Shin*
6. Back accompaniment of *shin*
7. Back accompaniment of *soe*
8. *Soe*
9. *Tai mikomi*

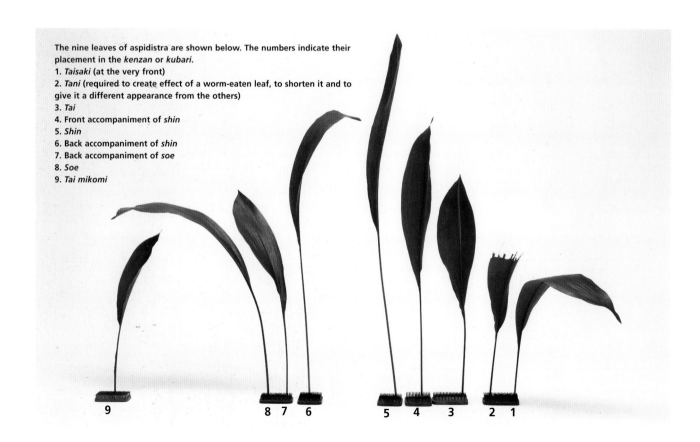

9   8 7 6   5 4 3   2 1

A complex richness in the guise of simplicity can be achieved by keeping to the basic concept of shin, soe, and taisaki, or "heaven, earth, and man," in an irregular triangular formation, and by adding accompaniments to each key position. To create such an arrangement, the Ikebana artist must have critical discernment, training, and technique. This method of combining materials, when skillfully employed, transforms simple line components—such as pussy willows, scotch broom, bulrushes, and others—into remarkable displays. This method of increasing the number of materials to accompany the basic structure is an ingenious organizational system for processing basic floral materials.

Using the diagram below as a guide, heaven = A, earth = B, and man = C. This forms an irregular triangle in Ikebana. However, if we then separate A, B, and C into independent units, the three parts of A become Aa, Ab, and Ac—thus, Aa = shin, Ab = back complement, and Ac = front complement. This single unit creates a triangular companionship.

Now subdivide further and within the back complement of B (still in the A unit): Ba = shin, Bb = back complement, and Bc = front complement for the B unit. In the front complement

of C (still in the A unit) Ca = shin, Cb = back complement, and Cc = front complement. This system, which can be applied to all of the units, allows you to increase numbers in a clear-cut orderly fashion. With this system, it's possible to imagine using thin line materials such as bulrushes for an arrangement. (See page 59 for an arrangement using bulrushes.)

Increasing numbers of materials can be added with this system, allowing you to create complex arrangements. When using branches that have many leaves and fine limbs, you can utilize this method for eliminating and adjusting elements in a systematic order. Sometimes in exhibitions, a seasoned Ikebana artist may display a Seika arrangement in line materials that appears to be simple, yet is dazzling in its enrichment because of the number of lines. As the viewer's eyes move from left to right and vice versa, the moiré effect gives an astonishing display of visual excitement. Such creations can be produced only with great patience and skill, as the artist controls the individual lines in precise order, without ever allowing the lines to cross in an X fashion. In addition, the same height in the individual materials should be avoided.

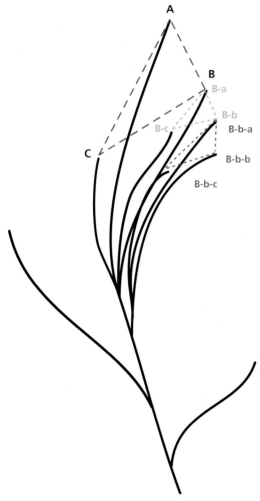

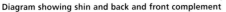

Diagram showing shin and back and front complement

Lessons in Moribana

Moribana is the first step to contemporary freestyle. In Moribana, the placement of the floral materials at the angles for each of the positions of shin, soe, and tai depends upon whether the arrangement is to be formal, semiformal, or informal. The circle in the diagram has been created for the convenience of the beginner.

A duplicate should be made of the circle, then it should be folded on the 90 degree line, with half of the circle pointing straight up. Then the viewer can see that the perpendicular line is 0 degrees. (These angles are quite different from plane geometry.)

Because flower arrangements are three-dimensional, shin at 10 degrees means it leans 10 degrees to the left or to the right of the perpendicular line of 0, and 10 degrees forward. Thus, in a left-hand pattern, shin will be 10 degrees left and forward. Shin at the 10 degrees position is maintained for all the formal-style arrangements in Moribana. However, soe and tai can move left or right and be lowered, depending upon the lines already present in the natural materials used. For this reason, each basic pattern has three variations. The diagrams on pages 169, 175 and 180–81 will help familiarize you with each of the variations.

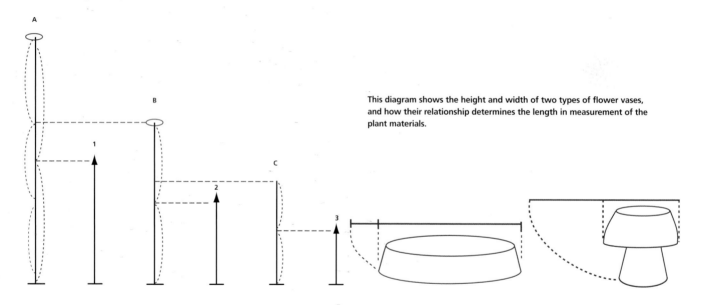

This diagram shows the height and width of two types of flower vases, and how their relationship determines the length in measurement of the plant materials.

Opposite: **Moribana in the formal basic style.** Vase: Ryusei School suiban in a dark-blue glaze. The simplicity of the upright lines in pussy willows makes them an ideal material for a beginner to use. Without the encumbrance of many limbs and leaves, pussy willows are durable and easy to bend, and their very simplicity can convey a great feeling of anticipation for new growth. *Shin*, the tallest pussy willow, is made into an elongated S-shape, but the top is left straight to create a sense of future growth. *Shin* is placed on the *kenzan* at center back (10 degrees to the left, 10 degrees forward). (See diagram of left-hand pattern basic style.) Next, *soe*, which is two-thirds the height of shin, is also shaped in an elongated S and is placed on the *kenzan* at left center (40 degrees to the left, 40 degrees forward). Tai, which appears to be short in the photo, is two-thirds of soe and is placed 70 degrees to the right and 50 to 60 degrees forward. The basic outline for an irregular (scalene) triangle is now completed. The complement flowers of yellow chrysanthemums are added next. As mentioned previously, when selecting chrysanthemums, it is important to look for blossoms that have the nicest leaves. In the Far East, the leaves of chrysanthemums are said to have medicinal powers and to promote longevity, so gardeners pay close attention to the care and nurturing of the leaves. If there is a selection, a mid-sized flower with a blossom that looks up should be used for the *shin* complement and should be one-half of *shin*. However, in this arrangement, because the chrysanthemums have so much more mass than the thin lines of pussy willows, the complement flowers are cut slightly shorter. The *shin* complement is placed on the *kenzan* immediately in front of *shin*. *Soe's* complement flower is a smaller blossom, one-half the length of soe or two-thirds of the *shin* complement, and is placed on the *kenzan* immediately to the right of *soe*, at center left. *Tai's* complement, one-half the length of *tai*, is placed at center front and is angled about 60 degrees. The angle of the lowest point of the complement flower should hide the *kenzan* from the viewer. If the arrangement is placed up higher, eye level will be higher, so the flower should be lower; if the placement is lower, the flower can be raised up. Its function is to obscure the *kenzan* from the viewer's sight.

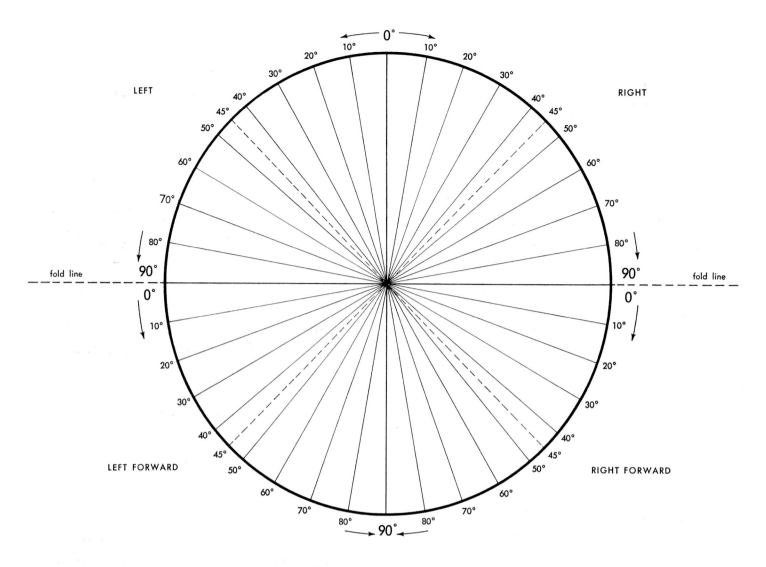

Diagram for angles in Ikebana

DETERMINING THE LENGTH OF MATERIALS

The diagram on page 166 shows the height and width of two types of flower vases and how the relationship between these dimensions determines the length of the plant materials. The height and width of the flower vase are added together to form a unit for measuring. The maximum length of the longest or tallest material you are planning to use in your arrangement should be 3 times that unit, even if you are using thin-line materials like pussy willows. If you are using more massive materials—those with many branches and leaves or flowers, such as gladiola—the measurement should be one and one-half to two times the unit length.

This measurement is for A, or shin.

Once you determine the height for A, it is always wise to add a couple of inches so that you have some leeway, since you may have to cut your materials several times during the process of arranging. Remember to take into account the depth of the flower vase.

Once A, or shin, has been decided, you can arrive at the length of B (soe) and C (tai). The measurement for B, or soe, will be two-thirds of shin, and C, or tai, will be two-thirds of B.

If A and B are branches, then the accompanying flower for A will be half of A; flower 2 will be half of B, and flower 3 will be half of C.

These convenient lengths or heights are for standard measurements. You may wish to use longer lengths for thin materials and shorter lengths for materials with more mass. These adjustments are based upon artistic judgment in measuring, not upon physical measurements. Also, because you must take into account the depth of the vase, and angle placement, you will have to adjust the length of the materials accordingly.

FORMAL, SEMIFORMAL, AND INFORMAL

In Moribana, kenzan style, the basic rule is that any part at a lower degree is placed toward the back. Accompanying materials are usually placed in the kenzan within the irregular triangular form of A, B, C. The exception is that accompanying materials at the very front will be placed on the A line. In the diagrams showing the kenzan placement, A = shin, B = soe, and C = tai. These diagrams show the shin, soe, and tai positions in the kenzan and the left-hand and right-hand patterns (a mirror image). Depending upon the materials you are using, you may have to readjust the pattern, but stay close to the percentages in the diagrams that follow.

FORMAL STYLE: BASIC AND ITS VARIATIONS

In the study of Moribana flower arrangements, one should begin with the basic formal category, which is the best introduction to the standard lengths, the bending and shaping of each plant, the placement in the kenzan for each position, and the total balance among the individual floral materials. These rules have been set up as a convenient reference for study.

THE BASIC STYLE

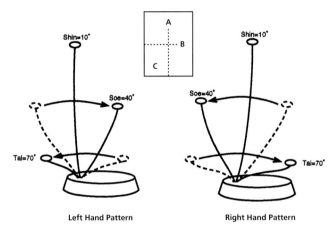

Left Hand Pattern   Right Hand Pattern

For the basic style, *shin* (A) will be placed at the center back of the *kenzan*: 10 degrees to the left and 10 degrees forward. *Soe* (B) will be placed 40 degrees to the left and 40 degrees forward. Tai (C) will be placed 70 degrees to the right and 70 degrees to the front. The rectangular diagram shows the positions on the *kenzan* for a left-hand pattern arrangement.

THE FIRST VARIATION

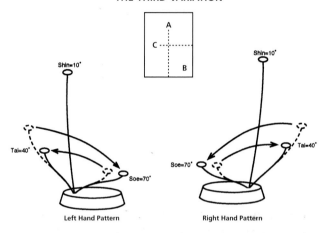

Left Hand Pattern   Right Hand Pattern

For the first variation, *shin* (A) remains at 10 degrees and *soe* (B) moves to the left front of the *kenzan*: 70 degrees down and 70 degrees forward. *Tai* (C) moves to the right-hand center of the *kenzan*: 40 degrees to the right and 40 degrees toward the front. The rectangular diagram shows the positions on the *kenzan* for a left-hand pattern arrangement.

THE SECOND VARIATION

Left Hand Pattern   Right Hand Pattern

For the second variation, *shin* (A) remains at 10 degrees and *soe* (B) moves to center right: 40 degrees to the right and 40 degrees forward. *Tai* (C) is at the left-front corner: 70 degrees to the left and 70 degrees forward. The rectangular diagram shows the positions on the *kenzan* for a left-hand pattern arrangement.

THE THIRD VARIATION

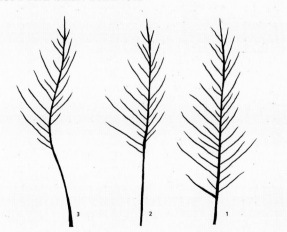

Left Hand Pattern   Right Hand Pattern

For the third variation, *shin* (A) remains the same. *Soe* (B) moves to the right-front corner: 70 degrees to the right and 45 degrees toward the front. *Tai* (C) is at the center left: 40 degrees to the left and 40 degrees toward the front. The rectangular diagram shows the positions on the *kenzan* for a left-hand pattern arrangement.

REMOVING EXCESS MATERIALS FROM THE SHIN BRANCH

If the materials have multiple branches, the arranger must determine which side of the branch would be ideal for the upper side. If the branch has leaves, it is easy to identify the front or back. Leaves that face the viewer or look up will always be the front. Otherwise, the branch should be carefully studied to see if the sub-branches could be utilized as the shin back and/or front complement. Also keep in mind that eventually the branch will be formed in a curvature of an elongated S-shape. While holding the branch, keep turning it around to see which lines would be most useful. Then follow steps 1, 2, and 3 in the diagram to get a clear understanding of which sub-branches should be removed to accommodate the complement flowers. The extended branches all around the lower part of the shin branch should be eliminated. These instructions apply to the Moribana, Nageire, and Seika styles of Ikebana.

Diagram showing removal of excess material from the *shin* branch for Moribana, Nageire, and Seika.

Above left: **Moribana: Formal style, second variation.** Vase: Contemporary suiban in blue glaze. When you make an arrangement, you must first take into account the materials on hand and the location and space where the arrangement will be placed. This will help determine whether the style of the arrangement will be formal, semiformal, or informal. This example is a formal arrangement in a right-hand pattern of the second variation. Mimosa acacia branches are used for *shin*, *soe*, and *tai*. Using the diagram of the *kenzan* for the second variation (see page 169), *shin*, A, is center back (10 degrees left and 10 degrees forward); *soe*, B, is right "horizontal" center (40 degrees right and 40 degrees forward); and *tai*, C, is in the left-front corner (70 degrees left and 45 to 50 degrees forward). The length of *shin* is slightly more than twice the width and height of vase. For a beginner in Moribana, it is easier to start with materials where *shin*, *soe*, and *tai* are single branches rather than "many line" materials. The natural curvature in materials can be utilized. In this case, the lower part of *soe* has an interesting curve, so, instead of the basic pattern, the arrangement uses the second variation. The *soe* complement flower, the tallest rose, fills in the space between *shin* and *soe*. The second rose is supposed to be the *soe* complement, but it is placed closer to the first rose for a more satisfactory sense of balance, instead of being placed at exactly the halfway point between *shin* and *tai*. A serene open space is created in this arrangement. Bouvardia flowers for *tai* are placed at center front on the *kenzan* to cover the *kenzan* from the viewer's sight. Taller bouvardia flowers fill the lower open space between the *soe* and *shin* group. The open surface of water in the *suiban* adds a pleasing dimension and also has an anchoring effect in this design, especially since *shin* is tilted to the left. The active empty space is designed to be over the surface of the water in the *suiban*.

Above right: **Moribana. Formal right-hand pattern, first variation.** Vase: Contemporary *suiban* in white and blue glaze. When using branches such as Chinese hawthorn, it is always wise to remove the limbs and leaves to about one-third of the lower part of *shin*. When you cut iris or any other floral materials, you should attempt to cut the stem without damaging the extra leaves, so that they may be used as additional materials. A branch of Chinese hawthorn for *shin* is placed at center back of the *kenzan* (10 degrees to the right and 10 degrees forward); the Chinese hawthorn *soe* moves to the left-front corner (70 degrees to the left and 45 to 50 degrees forward). The iris *tai* is placed in the center (40 degrees to the right and 30 degrees toward the front). A short branch of Chinese hawthorn is used to complement the *tai* iris. The tallest iris, the complement flower of *shin*, is placed to its left and is almost perpendicular. Pink chrysanthemums are used to fill in the lower part of the arrangement to cover the *kenzan*. Iris leaves, which have been carefully removed from the flower stem, are added to fill in space. After taking into consideration that the mass is in the lower part of this arrangement, in combination with the design and size of the flower vase, the *kenzan* is placed at the left front, so that the overall active empty space is above the vase. After you have completed an arrangement using a *suiban*, you should move the *kenzan* around to see what you feel is the best location, according to your artistic judgment. If you use some semipermanent substance, such as putty, for added stability, then you cannot readjust the *kenzan* placement.

Moribana: Formal right-hand pattern, first variation. Vase: Contemporary "compote style" suiban in yellow glaze. Nandina branches, stripped bare except for the top mass of leaves, form the interesting basic stems of *shin*, *soe*, and *tai* in this arrangement. *Shin* is placed on the *kenzan* at center back (10 degrees to the right and 10 degrees to the front). *Soe* is placed at the front-right corner (70 degrees to the right, 40 to 45 degrees to front). *Tai* is placed on the left center of the *kenzan* (40 degrees to the left and 40 degrees forward). The *shin* complement flower, narcissus, is about one-half the height of *shin* and is placed right in front of *shin* on the *kenzan*; it then moves straight up to the left in a perpendicular line. The *soe* complement narcissus, half the length of *soe*, is placed to the right of the *shin* narcissus. Usually, the *soe* complement is supposed to be placed at center front and lean toward the viewer at about a 60-degree angle; however, the natural characteristic of narcissus is to stand upright. Variations such as this are the first step toward the creation of freestyle arrangements in natura-listic Moribana. Chrysanthemums are used as *tai* complements and to fill the lower space and cover the *kenzan*. *Note:* The leaves and stems of narcissus are eas-ily damaged when placed on the *kenzan*. To keep them from gradually falling over, it is wise to wrap the lower stem with vinyl tape.

Moribana: First step to freestyle. Vase: Yellow glazed ceramic. The placement of the tallest horsetail (*Equisetum*) can be perceived as a formal *shin*. Then multiple shorter horsetails positioned in a somewhat two-dimensional manner. To enhance this two-dimensional aspect, the three horsetails are bent to encapsulate the structure. Once the composition of *Equisetum* has been completed, the orange lilies are placed at the lower left to visually anchor the arrangement. Finally, purple bachelor's buttons are placed in higher positions to provide accent among the lines of a two-dimensional composition. Finally, in examining this composition, use your imagination or cover the top line of the tallest horsetail and see how the composition changes. Thus, you can see how the fundamental patterns of *shin*, *soe*, and *tai* can be eventually overruled, once you have developed your own imaginative composition.

Above, left: **Moribana: First step to freestyle.** Vase: Contemporary ceramic vase. This is a lesson in creating a freestyle arrangement. Begin by using the *shin* angle from the basic style as a first step. Then use your artistic senses to guide you as you add the other materials, without concern for the exact placement of the *soe* and *tai* positions. The tallest freesia is placed center back on the *kenzan* (10 degrees to the left, 10 degrees forward) in a formal left-hand pattern style. The second and third freesias are then placed to form a group of freesias. Since freesia stems are straight, fasciated Scotch broom, with its characteristic curvatures, is added to provide a sense of movement. Pussy willows are added to create an overall sense of balance. The lower white, lacy umbel flowers (members of the parsnip family) fill in spaces in between other plant materials and cover the *kenzan*. Please notice the curvatures of the fasciated Scotch broom—how they seem to reverberate in "echoes" with each other and are dominant in line movement. The three yellow freesias suggest a vision of spring.

Above, right: **Moribana: First step to freestyle.** Vase: Contemporary *suiban* in light-blue glaze. Eulalia grass (*Miscanthus zebrinus*) is placed in the *shin* position as in a left-hand pattern style (10 degrees left and 10 degrees forward). The graceful curves of the leaf blades are echoed by the curved stems of yellow patrinia. The patrinia to the right of the eulalia grass creates an irregular, or scalene, triangle with the one to the left and the lowest of the short patrinia. The fourth patrinia to the left of the tall one is used as filler. The lowest chrysanthemum flower and leaves cover the *kenzan*. The upper chrysanthemum stem adds balance and texture. The lower eulalia grass fills space and reflects the main eulalia grass. Although this is a move away from basic patterns, it is easier and wiser to utilize some of the fundamental structures such as shin, soe, and tai. You may veer from the exact length and angle, but prior knowledge of the basics is very helpful for creating a freestyle arrangement in a naturalistic manner. Freestyle can roughly be divided into two categories: one is naturalistic, and the other is abstract. Naturalistic means, for example, that the eulalia grass will be used as it grows in nature. Abstract, on the other hand, means that the arranger may take a group of eulalia stems as line material and then roll, wire, and form them into a circular structure with multiple lines. While the results are totally different in appearance, it is still the same material.

SEMIFORMAL STYLE: BASIC AND ITS VARIATIONS

By utilizing these angles for your materials, and by bringing each material forward, you will create three-dimensionality in your arrangements. Often, beginners will create fan-shaped two-dimensional arrangements. Pay attention to the relationships among A, B, and C and the "active empty" spaces in between.

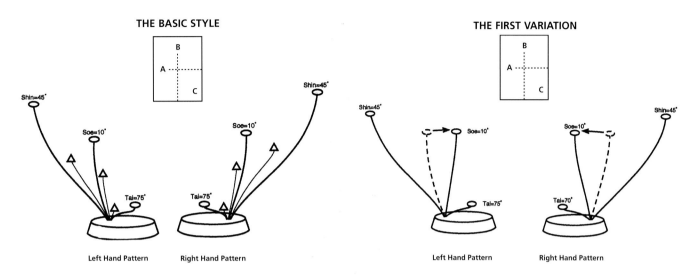

THE BASIC STYLE

Left Hand Pattern   Right Hand Pattern

THE FIRST VARIATION

Left Hand Pattern   Right Hand Pattern

For the basic style, *shin* (A) will be placed at the center back of the *kenzan*, 45 degrees to the left and 45 degrees forward. *Soe* (B) will be placed 10 degrees to the left and 10 degrees forward. *Tai* (C) will be placed 75 degrees to the right and 70 degrees to the front. The rectangular diagram shows the positions on the *kenzan* for a left-hand pattern arrangement.

For the first variation, *shin* (A) remains at 45 degrees and *soe* (B) remains at the center back of the *kenzan*: 10 degrees down and 10 degrees forward. *Tai* (C) moves to the right-hand center of the *kenzan*: 75 degrees to the right and 70 degrees toward the front. The rectangular diagram shows the positions on the *kenzan* for a left-hand pattern arrangement.

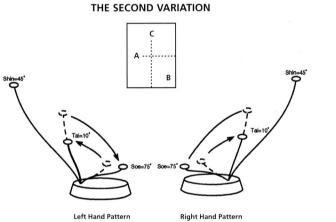

THE SECOND VARIATION

Left Hand Pattern   Right Hand Pattern

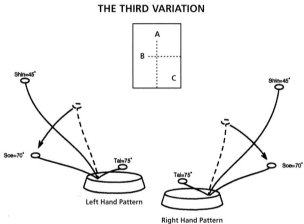

THE THIRD VARIATION

Left Hand Pattern

Right Hand Pattern

For the second variation, *shin* (A) remains at 45 degrees and *soe* (B) moves to the right-front corner: 75 degrees to the right and 40 degrees forward. *Tai* (C) is at the center back: 10 degrees to the left and 10 degrees forward. The rectangular diagram shows the positions on the *kenzan* for a left-hand pattern arrangement.

For the third variation, shin (A) moves to the center back, remaining at 45 degrees. *Soe* (B) moves to the left center: 70 degrees to the left and 70 degrees toward the front. *Tai* (C) is at the right-front corner: 75 degrees to the right and 75 degrees forward. The rectangular diagram shows the positions on the *kenzan* for a left-hand pattern arrangement.

Left: **Moribana: Formal left-hand pattern, first variation.** Vase: Contemporary *suiban* with legs. A practitioner of Ikebana art, over the years, can eventually develop a powerful sense of organization that can be transferred to other art forms. A trained eye will immediately recognize the dominant subject and then make decisions about what other elements are necessary to complete the work of art. Elimination is also important to enhance the dominant subject. This exercise is a lesson in how to remove unnecessary or interfering limbs and leaves, so that each material has its own domain and space. (The floral materials should never contact the edge of the flower vase.) In this arrangement, podocarpus branches are used for shin, soe, and tai. Because podocarpus branches have many smaller limbs and leaves, they are very good materials for beginners to study. One must decide which limbs and leaves should be removed, which should be saved for further consideration, and which should be used to delineate and define the main lines. It is also necessary to decide how to create space for the complement flowers. Carefully study the main branches, then begin eliminating unnecessary limbs and leaves. Everything from the lower half of each branch should be removed. It is important to cut your floral materials slightly longer than the desired length, so you will have some leeway, if you should need to do some trimming later on. On the *shin* branch, remove the limbs and leaves on the lower half of the right-hand side to make space for the *shin* complement flower, and then proceed to gently shape the desired curve of the branch. *Shin* will be placed at the center back of the *kenzan* (10 degrees to the left and 10 degrees forward). The *soe* branch will be placed in the front-left corner (70 degrees to the left, 50 to 60 degrees forward). The *soe* branch should be two-thirds of *shin*. The *tai* branch will be two-thirds of *soe* and placed at center right (40 degree right, 40 degrees forward). The *shin* complement chrysanthemum, one-half of *shin*, will be placed on the *kenzan* immediately in front of *shin*. The soe complement, one-half of *soe*, will be placed on the *kenzan* at the left-hand center (40 degrees left, 45 to 50 degrees forward). The *tai* complement of small pink chrysanthemums will fill the lower part, to cover the *kenzan*.

Above: **Moribana: Semiformal left-hand pattern, second variation.** Vase: Ryusei School *suiban* with a light-blue glaze. Materials such as raspberry branches are difficult to bend and, therefore, it is important to utilize the naturally attached limbs as part of the design. Selectively and carefully remove some of the lower limbs and leaves, especially from the underside of the branch, from the midpoint of *shin* downward. The elimination of limbs from the lower part of the branch and the underside of the branch is common practice. For this naturalistic arrangement, shin is placed on the kenzan at left center (45 degrees to the left, 45 degrees forward); *soe* is in the right-front corner (75 degrees to the right and forward 50 to 60 degrees); and *tai* is at center back (10 degrees to the left, 10 degrees forward). In the photograph, *tai* appears deceptively short, but in reality, it is two-thirds of *soe*. The complement flowers for *shin* are yellow chrysan-themums, which come up to the midpoint of *shin*'s height, and are placed on the *kenzan* immediately to the right of it. The *soe* complement, also one-half of *soe*, is placed at center front. In this arrangement, the *soe* group leans forward and opens up the space behind. Therefore, to fill in the space artistically, the *tai* complement flowers are the fringed pinks. The many stems and blossoms make these flowers perfect for filling in the space. Additional small branches are added between *shin* and *tai* to fill in space. In this arrangement, the *kenzan* is also placed at the right side of the *suiban*, because *soe* extends to the right in a lower position. This opens up the active empty space so that it is directly above the *suiban*.

Left, top: **Moribana: Semiformal right-hand pattern, basic style.** Vase: Ryusei School suiban with a tan glaze. In this right-hand pattern, fasciated Scotch broom is *shin* and is 45 degrees to the right and 45 degrees forward; *soe* is 10 degrees to the right and 10 degrees back; and *tai* is 75 degrees to the left and 75 degrees forward. In the photograph, *tai* appears disproportionately short, but in reality, it is two-thirds the length of *soe*. While Scotch broom and willow are quite common and can be found in most floral markets, their fasciated varieties are much more difficult to find. This arrangement, however, can be created with common Scotch broom. Scotch broom is very easy to handle and can take bending and curving quite easily. Each branch has masses of wandlike green stems with very tiny leaves. With patience, you can align the stems to create a smooth movement. Do your best to avoid crossing lines. Form a stretched S-line with multiple lines to give a pleasing effect. The *shin* complement rose is placed next to it, on the left; the *soe* complement will be placed in front of it on the *kenzan*; the *tai* complement, which is the largest blossom, will be placed at the center front of the *kenzan*. The size of the blossom is not necessarily intended to cover the *kenzan*, but to give visual stability and provide an anchoring effect. When the *shin*, *soe*, and *tai* materials have dramatic curvatures, often beginners will have difficulty determining the angles to use. In such cases, draw an imaginary line from the tip to the bottom end, and create the angle on that line, rather than on the stem. Always make sure that the tip curvature or other special features are utilized effectively. When using this type of flat vase, or *suiban*, the placement of the *kenzan* is important. The active empty space should be right above the center of the *suiban*.

Left, bottom: **Moribana: Semiformal left-hand pattern, first variation.** Vase: Ryusei School *suiban* in dark-blue glaze. New Zealand flax (*Phormiun tenax*) is another plant that is commonly found in floral markets. The sharp and simple lines in an arrangement provide contrast for most flowers. In this arrangement, *shin* is 45 degrees to the left and 45 degrees to the front; *soe* moves to the right (10 degrees forward, 10 degrees right); and *tai* is 75 degrees to the right and about 60 to 70 degrees forward. Such materials as New Zealand flax have thin leaf blades, so depending upon the type of *kenzan* you use, the leaf may not hold the desired angle. If such is the case, use short pieces of the excess leaves that have been cut off and sandwich them inside the fold of the leaf to add girth; then, cut the bottom of the leaf unit at an angle. The red dahlias are used as complement flowers. Bleached and dried ferns are used to fill in spaces where necessary. For the complements, if you have a selection of the same flower, save the largest blossom for the bottom, the medium one for the shin com-plement, and the smallest for the soe complement. Please pay attention to the placement of the kenzan. Because this is the first variation, the *soe* moves to the right 10 degrees, and the open space between *shin* and *soe* is much larger, thus creating active empty space right over the suiban when the *kenzan* is placed at the extreme right. Please compare this arrangement with the basic style in the arrangement show on page 158.

Moribana: Semiformal left-hand pattern, freestyle. Vase: Contemporary ceramic, compote style, with a white glaze. In this example of a semiformal right-hand arrangement, the tallest spike flower, as *shin*, is placed 45 degrees to the left and 45 degrees forward. Below *shin*, the *soe* spike flower is placed in the position shown in the third variation (see the diagram on page 180). Two more spike flowers are added. The white gentians appear to be shin complements, but the direction and length of all the materials are probably free, following to the arranger's artistic sense. The blades of the long leaves provide smooth, curving lines. The mass created by the flowers in the lower center gives a sense of stability to this wide-open composition. The white gentians both complement and enhance the white contemporary ceramic vase. This is a naturalistic freestyle arrangement.

Right, top: **Moribana: Semiformal left-hand pattern, third variation.** Vase: Contemporary suiban in dark-blue glaze. In this third variation in a semiformal pattern, eucalyptus branches are used for *shin*, *soe*, and *tai*. When *soe*, which is next in length to *shin*, is moved in the same direction, a great sense of one-directional movement is created. For this reason, *tai* is not composed of the same material as *shin* and *soe*. To enhance the sense of direction, *shin* now moves to the center back (45 degrees left, 30 degrees forward) of the *kenzan*. *Note:* Whatever the number of degrees may be, the lowest number always goes back, and the highest number comes forward on the *kenzan*. Soe is placed to the far left (70 degrees at left center, 30 to 35 degrees forward). The poppy, as *tai*, is placed at the right-front corner (75 degrees to the right and 60 to 70 degrees forward). (Again, in the photograph, this *tai* poppy appears deceptively short but is in fact two-thirds of soe.) The complement flower for *shin*, the tallest poppy with a bud (half the height of *shin*), is placed right in front of *shin* but is angled so that it is almost perpendicular. The *soe* complement is placed to the right, but it is angled between the *shin* and *soe* branches. The tai complement is the most open flower at the center front. Additional eucalyptus branches are added to enhance the curvature for a left-directional movement. Small white daisies are used to fill space. Although the total concept in design is one-directional to the left, both tips of the *shin* and *soe* lines give hints of upward movement. The direction that the poppy blossoms face also keeps the direction in balance. This treatment of the ends of shin and soe lines is important in naturalistic arrangement because it suggests the life force or vitality of the plants and hints at further growth. Although the materials have been cut, this illusion of growth is the essence of creativity in Ikebana art.

Right, bottom: **Moribana: Semiformal free arrangement.** Vase: Contemporary ceramic with a dark-blue glaze. The most dominating branch on the far left is placed at an angle (45 degrees left and 45 degrees forward). The secondary branch, as *soe*, is placed at 70 degrees to the left and 60 degrees forward. This pattern is in the third variation, semiformal style (see the diagram on page 180). The branch to the far right is added to break away from the formally set pattern of the third variation. All these choices of positions and angles for the floral materials are based on the desire to fully utilize the natural lines and directions of each plant. The flower complements no longer serve as *shin* complement or *soe* complement but are placed on the *kenzan* in a much freer manner. The yellow chrysanthemums give a nice accent, in contrast to the Turkish balloon flowers, and echo the color of the leaf buds on the branches. The reasonably straight branch next to *shin* fills in the open space between the two tall branches. This is a good example of the way fundamental patterns can be utilized as a beginning point in your creative arrangements. The dark-blue ceramic vase appears to give energy to the dark stems of the branches. The tight leaf buds suggest the future and vibrate with the energy of their life force.

INFORMAL STYLE: BASIC AND ITS VARIATIONS

It is important to note that the third variation in the informal style is the first time that the materials lean toward the back. Some of the flowers or branches have interesting curvatures at the end; these should be placed so that the "face" looks forward. These diagrams and directions are intended to help the novice Ikebana arranger more easily understand and learn the art. Your pattern selection will depend upon the space in which your arrangement will be displayed, or upon the characteristics of the materials you have on hand, or both. Depending on these factors, you may choose formal, semiformal, or informal styles. For a centerpiece on a table, you might try using these variations back to back, with slight artistic adjustments, to allow for a 360-degree view. The rectangular diagrams show the position on the kenzan for a left-hand pattern arrangement.

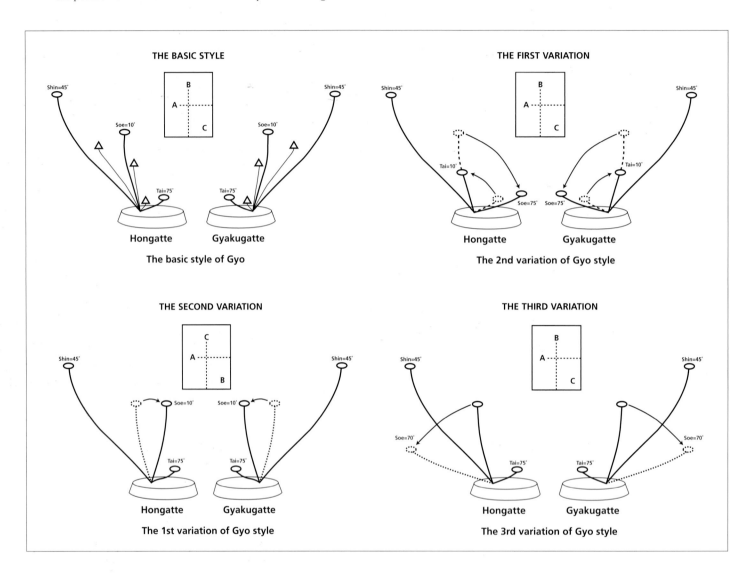

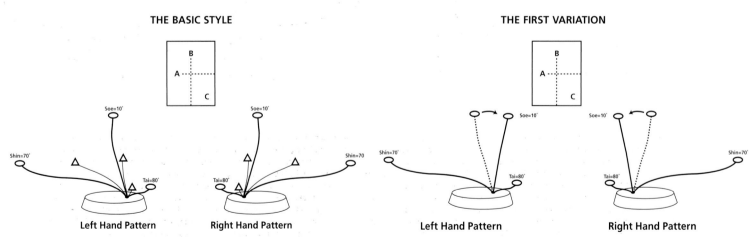

THE SECOND VARIATION

Left Hand Pattern

Right Hand Pattern

THE THIRD VARIATION

Left Hand Pattern

Right Hand Pattern

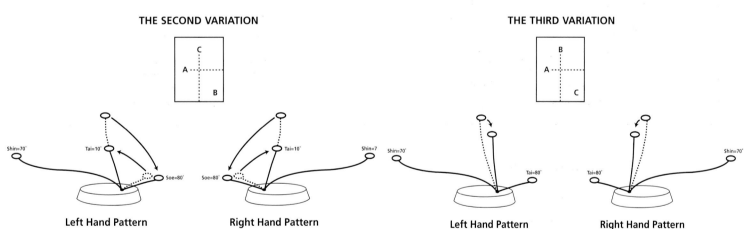

Above: **Moribana: Informal, basic pattern.** Vase: Contemporary rectangular ceramic suiban with a blue glaze. A characteristic of this informal style is that shin leans down for a 70 degree angle. For this reason, the flower vase is usually in a flat oblong shape. Early spring hydrangea branches, which have been stripped bare except for the few new leaves at the tips, are used for *shin*, *soe*, and *tai*. Hydrangea branches are difficult to bend and shape, but they do have unique natural curves that can be skillfully utilized. This arrangement is a lesson on how to make the most of these natural curves. Because this is in the natura-listic style of Moribana, the tips of the lines should face upward to impart a sense of the force of life. *Shin*, which appears to be almost horizontal, is placed at an angle of 75 degrees, to the right of *soe*. *Soe*, which is two-thirds the length of *shin*, is placed at the back center of the *kenzan*, at a 10 degree angle to the right and 10 degrees forward. *Tai*, which is two-thirds of *soe*, is placed at a 75 degree angle to the left and about 70 degrees forward. Because of the angle of *tai*, which leans forward, it appears to be much shorter in the photograph than it is in reality. Blue ribbon iris as the shin complement is about half of *shin* and is placed at the center, right next to *shin*. Depending upon the size of the *kenzan* one uses, this extreme angle may need a counterbalanced *kenzan* placed upside down at one end (see page 148). The *soe* complement is half of *soe*, placed immediately to the left of *soe*, at the center back of the *kenzan*. White daisies are used as *tai* complements and are placed at the center front. Additional daisies fill the space. If one makes good use of the natural lines of these sim-ple smooth-line materials, then quite an uplifting feeling can be created. Since the important open space is directly above the flowers, the *kenzan* is placed at the far left. The reflection of flowers on the water's surface is, as always, a beautiful effect.

Moribana: Informal right-hand pattern, first variation. Vase: Contemporary ceramic, rectangular suiban with a blue glaze. The main branches for this arrangement are forsythia. The placement for *shin* is at the left center of the *kenzan* (70 degree left, 40 degree forward); the placement for *soe*, which is two-thirds the length of *shin*, is center back (10 degree to right; 10 degrees forward); and *tai*, which is two-thirds of *soe*, is placed at the right-hand front corner (80 degrees to the right, 50 to 60 degrees forward). *Tai* appears disproportionately shorter in the photograph because of its angle. The *shin* complement Chinese bellflower, which is half the length of *shin*, is, in this case, the largest blossom used. It is placed on the *kenzan* right next to *shin*. The *soe* complement, half of *soe*, is placed on the *kenzan* right in front of the *soe* branch and is almost perpendicular. Please notice the direction that the flowers face. The *tai* complement is the white chrysanthemum that is placed at the center front of the *kenzan*. Additional white mums, Chinese bellflowers, and short forsythia branches fill in the space.

Moribana: Informal left-hand pattern, second variation. Vase: Contemporary ceramic, compote style, with a turquoise glaze. A palm leaf is used for the main position of *shin* in this second variation arrangement. *Shin* is placed at an angle of 70 degrees at the left center of the *kenzan* and leans 30 degrees forward. White daisies, as soe, are placed on the *kenzan* at the right-front corner and are angled 80 degrees to the right and 60 to 70 degrees forward. Pink carnations, as *tai*, are placed at the center back of the *kenzan* and are angled 10 degrees to the left and 10 degrees forward. In this informal variation arrangement, much freer usage is allowed; however, soe appears to be much shorter only because of the camera angle. The extended line to the left becomes the dominating visual effect. Additional palm leaves placed in the center lean toward the left, emphasizing a one-sided concept in design. Pink carnations and shorter white daisies form the mass for maintaining balance.

Moribana: Using the left-hand pattern for a freestyle arrangement. Vase: Brown-glazed contemporary ceramic rectangular suiban. In this arrangement, early spring Japanese dogwood branches, still with tight leaf buds, are used for *shin* and *soe*. Shin is placed at center right on the *kenzan*, 70 degrees to the right and 40 degrees forward. *Soe* is placed at the center back. In a traditional arrangement, the forked branch to the left on the main *soe* branch would have been eliminated; however, its movement is a beautiful echo to that of the *shin* branch. This is a first step to creating a freestyle arrangement. Depending upon the materials you have on hand, if nature should supply a line that provides additional enhancement, it should be utilized. A large tulip leaf is used for *tai*, which is placed in the left-front corner of the *kenzan* (80 degrees to the left, 70 to 75 degrees forward). It is very difficult to place red tulips at an angle, and their dramatic presence would overshadow the movement of the branches; therefore, small yellow chrysanthemums are used for the shin complement. The tulips are placed upright as the *soe* complement. Because this approach is more of a freestyle, the *shin* complement is shorter. The *tai* complement is placed at the front center and comes straight forward to cover the *kenzan*. In this arrangement, the usually dominant *shin* unit takes a subdominant position to the *soe* unit, with its red tulips, which now become the dominant presence.

Moribana: Informal left-hand pattern, third variation. Vase: Contemporary ceramic, compote style, with a yellow glaze. Spirea branches are used for the main positions in this arrangement. Most spirea branches will have many secondary branches, so judicious care must be given to the selection for removal. The third variation is the most unusual in the category of Moribana. In most of the arrangement patterns for the examples shown so far, all of the plant materials leaned toward the front. But in this case, *soe*, the second-longest branch, which is placed at the center back of the *kenzan*, leans straight back 35 degrees. This effect makes the arrangement more flat. *Shin* is placed on the *kenzan* center left, and is angled at 70 degrees to the left and 30 degrees forward. *Tai* is angled 80 degrees to the right. Tulips are the complement flowers for *shin* and *soe*, and white daisies are the complement for tai. This arrangement, with its contrast of light and dark pink tulips, small and large white daisies, and spirea flowers in a yellow vase, exudes an atmosphere of the freshness and light-heartedness of early spring.

Lessons in Nageire

In many ways, the development of Ikebana is a story of the relationship of materials to their container. From this point of view, the significant difference between Rikka, Seika, and Moribana, on the one hand, and Nageire and its offspring Chabana, on the other, is that the first three styles are freestanding within the vase, while Nageire and Chabana arrangements will lean against the mouth of the vase.

Compared to Rikka, Seika, and Moribana, Nageire is much more "arranger-friendly." In Nageire, and the related Chabana, materials can be placed in a vase to make an arrangement without the use of a freestanding holder. Today, the Nageire form of Ikebana is becoming more prevalent and accepted by the public.

Cut branches and flowers must be put in water immediately to preserve their freshness, so that they may be enjoyed for a longer period of time. To display them to their best advantage, branches of flowering plum, with their wonderful fragrance, or gorgeous cherry blossoms, for example, would be most suitably placed in a tall upright container or laid horizontally in a flat one. However, each branch has its individual curvature and weight, and its natural tendency to turn for balance may not leave it in the ideal position for the viewer to enjoy its beauty.

Left: **Nageire: Formal right-hand pattern, first variation.** Vase: Contemporary ceramic with a jarlike opening. Young raspberry branches were stripped relatively bare so that the lines of the three main positions would be clearly exposed for lesson purposes. *Shin* is placed at 10 degrees to the right and 10 degrees forward. (Note: You may have to add a section of a discarded branch to the bottom of *shin* to obtain the proper height.) *Soe* is 40 degrees to the left and 40 degrees forward. *Soe*, when placed in the vase, will rest on the left-front corner of the rim. The lower part of the branch is forcibly broken to maintain the angle, and four or five inches of the stem will go straight down. The break in the branch will be in contact with the inner side and will help to sustain the upper part of the branch in the desired direction. If you look down at the vase and imagine a clock face on the rim, with 6:00 o'clock being in front, the contact point of the *soe* break is at the 2:00 o'clock position, and the branch leans against the rim at the 7:00 o'clock position. Hold the *tai* branch up to the vase for the required length, then break the stem just as you broke the stem for *soe*. *Tai* is 70 degrees to the right and 45 to 50 degrees to the front. A yellow lily as the complement flower is placed next to *shin* on its left. You may need additional length for this flower also. The second lily, half of *soe*, is inserted next to *soe*. Because visually lilies have more mass, as complement flowers, they are cut slightly shorter than required. Fringed pinks are the *tai* complement. The lower flower appears to be horizontal in placement. Flowers in the carnation or pink family have somewhat brittle stems, especially where leaves are attached, so the stems should be bent between the leaves. Be aware that because the angle of *tai* is extreme, a substantial length beyond the broken point is needed in the vase to serve as an anchor, or it will not hold; therefore, make sure you have ample length. This is especially so if the material happens to have many leaves or branches.

Opposite: **Nageire: Semiformal right-hand pattern, second variation.** Vase: White-glazed ceramic designed by the Ryusei School. These basic lessons will help you to clearly understand the proper use of angles and proportions. To hold certain angles, the lower portion of the stem, which is in the vase, is broken. Please refer to the photograph on page 152, which will show you the cross-shaped branch pieces that have been forcibly inserted into the vase to hold the plant materials. Use only one of the quarter sections to hold all of your plant materials in the arrangement. In this second variation, raspberry branches are used for the three positions. *Shin* is placed at 45 degrees to the right and 45 degrees forward. *Soe* is angled 80 degrees to the right and 60 to 70 degrees forward. (*Soe*, which is two-thirds of *shin*, appears to be deceptively short because of the photographic angle.) *Tai*, which is two-thirds of *soe*, leans 10 degrees to the right. The white gentian is the *shin* complement, and the yellow lily is the *soe* complement. Directly behind the *soe* complement is the white gentian for the *tai* complement.

FORMAL STYLE

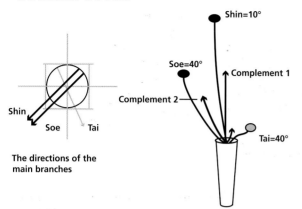

The directions of the main branches

The formal basic style: The throw-in method, in a left-hand pattern

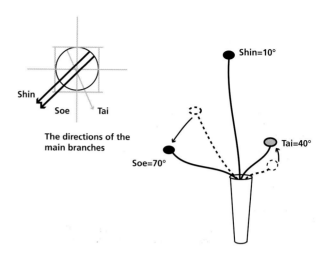

The directions of the main branches

The thrown-in method, in a left-hand pattern

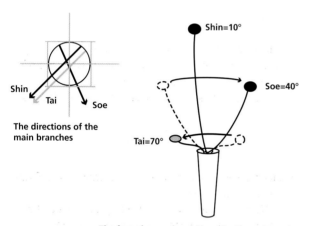

The directions of the main branches

The formal second variation: The throw-in method, in a left-hand pattern

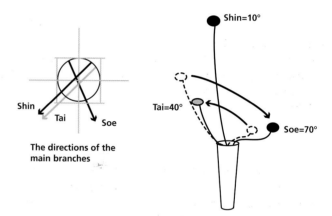

The directions of the main branches

The formal third variation: The throw-in method, in a left-hand pattern

SEMIFORMAL STYLE

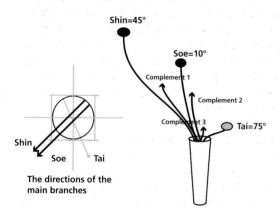

The directions of the main branches

The semiformal basic style: The throw-in method in a left-hand pattern

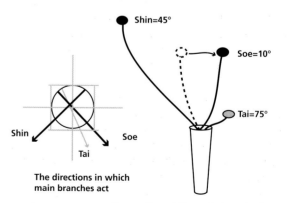

The directions in which main branches act

The semiformal first variation: The throw-in method in a left-hand pattern

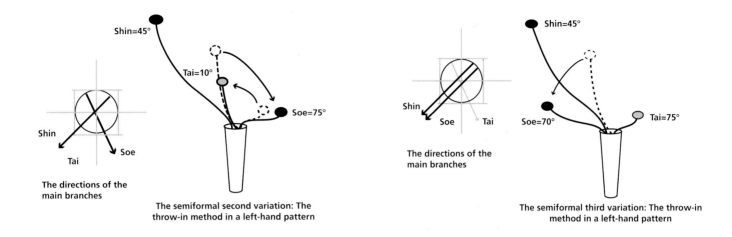

The directions of the
main branches

The semiformal second variation: The
throw-in method in a left-hand pattern

The directions of the
main branches

The semiformal third variation: The throw-in
method in a left-hand pattern

VASES FOR NAGEIRE

If you are not enrolled in an Ikebana class in Nageire, which would provide you with standard Nageire flower vases for lessons, you may have to improvise with certain techniques for maintaining the materials at an angle, after you study the basic techniques. The common Nageire flower vase is a tubular form, as seen in the following photographs of Nageire arrangements. However, any size and shape–spherical, oval, square, triangular, etc.–can be used. The Nageire technique is basic, and you can improvise using many different types of containers.

Along with the offerings to the Buddha of blossoms float-ing on water, floral materials displayed in a tall vase formed the foundation for the Nageire technique. Gradually, from very early days, skills for arranging floral materials in Nageire were developed. Techniques such as partially breaking or bending stems to sustain the direction of the branch were devised. The simple physics of weight, balance, and direction was taken into consideration.

The popularity of Nageire eventually led to the establish-ment of a school focusing only on the Nageire technique. The Nageire arrangements range from very large compositions to fill greater spaces to a simple one-flower, one-branch style. Today most of the schools of Ikebana use a kenzan, yet the fundamental techniques for Nageire are an essential study for any student of flower arranging.

In classic Ikebana, various techniques are used to make all of the floral materials stand upright from the center of the flower vase; in Moribana, a kenzan and other related equip-ment or tools are used so that the branches and flowers can be arranged at the desired angle. However, another set of tech-niques is used for Nageire. The first is the selection of the appropriate type of vase for the floral materials. The size and weight of the floral materials will help determine the height and width of the vase to be used. To make the floral material stand in the desired position, some elementary principles of the dynamics of physics must be considered. The floral mate-rials may flip and turn in the wrong direction, and there are methods for dealing with this problem (see pages 152–53). To make the study of the Nageire category more effective, the

fundamental patterns of the formal, semiformal, and informal styles are illustrated here.

In Nageire, the technique for holding materials at the desired angle does not depend upon the use of a kenzan; however, the proportions of height and angles for the individ-ual parts remain the same, for the formal and semiformal styles. In Nageire arrangements, according to the size and type of the flower vase, you may have to add length to the materials. For instance, suppose you need to maintain shin in an upright position in a formal pattern, but the stem does not reach the bottom. You may need to make an adjustment by adding an extension to the stem. If the material is to be placed at an angle, the end of the stem can contact the inner surface of the vase, providing that you have sufficient length. However, depending upon the shape of the vase, the floral material may or may not hold in that position, and again an adjustment may be needed.

In comparison with Moribana, in the Nageire informal style, because the vase is tall, the shin material can "drape" down at a 45 degree angle and effectively express seasonal richness, especially when branches with fruit such as pome-granates, persimmons, tangerines, and so on, are used.

For common practices to obtain the required angles and spacing in Nageire arrangements, as well as to control floral materials that are inclined to flip in the wrong direction, see pages 152–53 in the "Basic Ikebana Techniques" chapter. Nageire lesson patterns and steps are similar to those of Moribana; therefore, there will only be one example for each of the formal and semiformal patterns in this section.

Nageire: Informal basic left-hand pattern. Vase: Blue-glazed Nageire ceramic, designed by the Ryusei School. Forsythia branches are used for the three main positions in this arrangement. Unique to the informal style in Nageire is that *shin*, the dominant branch, sweeps down at an angle 45 degrees from the tall vase and leans 45 degrees forward. Simple line materials such as these forsythia branches are good for lessons because they are easy to bend in a natural way. *Soe*, the second longest material, is 10 degrees to the left and 20 degrees forward. *Tai* is 75 degrees to the right and 75 degrees forward. Pink roses are used as the complement flowers for *shin*, *soe*, and *tai*. The cluster of small yellow blossoms fills the center part. In this third variation pattern, in which *shin* sweeps down, branches that have fruits such as tangerines, persimmons, pomegranates, and the like would be ideal for an arrangement.

INFORMAL STYLE

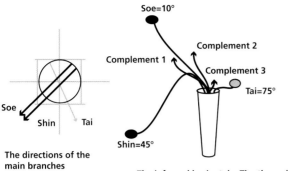

Soe=10°

Complement 2

Complement 1

Complement 3

Tai=75°

Shin=45°

Soe

Shin

Tai

The directions of the
main branches

The informal basic style: The throw-in
method in a left-hand pattern

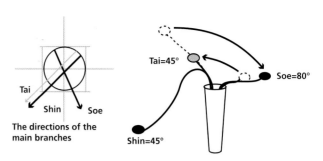

Tai=45°

Soe=80°

Shin=45°

Tai

Shin

Soe

The directions of the
main branches

The informal second variation: The throw-in
method in a left-hand pattern

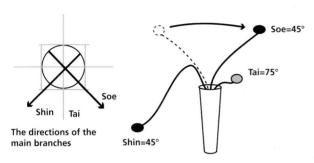

Soe=45°

Tai=75°

Shin=45°

Soe

Shin

Tai

The directions of the
main branches

The informal first variation: The throw-in
method in a left-hand pattern

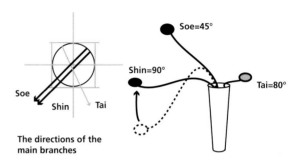

Soe=45°

Shin=90°

Tai=80°

Soe

Shin

Tai

The directions of the
main branches

The informal third variation: The throw-in
method in a left-hand pattern

Nageire: Informal style, first variation. Vase: Contemporary Nageire ceramic with a turquoise blue glaze. Branches of fasciated Scotch broom are used for the three main positions in this Nageire first variation arrangement. *Soe* now moves from the left to the right-hand side, at an angle 45 degrees to the right and 45 degrees forward. *Shin* is angled 45 degrees forward and then sweeps down. *Tai* is angled at 75 degrees to the right and 50 to 60 degrees forward. Orange lilies and yellow chrysanthemums serve as the complement flowers.

Nageire: Informal, second variation. Vase: White porcelain, styled after an ancient wine goblet of the Tang dynasty. Forsythia branches are used for the main positions in this Informal second variation arrangement. *Soe* is moved dramatically, 80 degrees to the right and 60 to 70 degrees forward. Because of the photographic angle, the full length of *soe* cannot be seen. Purple gentians and yellow patrinia provide a nice contrast in color and texture.

Nageire: Informal left-hand pattern, third variation. Vase: Ceramic with a blue glaze. In another version of the third variation informal style, the placement of *shin* becomes a horizontal line. The placement of *shin* is now horizontal, 90 degrees right and 30 degrees forward; *soe* is 45 degrees to the right and 20 degrees forward; and *tai* is 80 degrees to the left and 80 degrees forward. *Tai* is two-thirds of *soe*, although in the photograph, because of the angle, it appears to be shorter. Raspberry branches are used for the main lines in this arrangement. Nature has provided a complement branch in *shin*, which is well utilized. The limb attached at a lower point of the *soe* branch, under the chrysanthemum, appears as the *shin* complement. The pink chrysanthemum as the *shin* complement is half of *shin*. In this arrangement, to enhance the one-directional movement, the second pink chrysanthemum is used as a *tai* complement, rather than as an upright *soe* complement flower. Along with the *soe* complement, white daisies are added to fill space. These adjustments and changes in the complementary floral materials are the first step to creating freestyle arrangements. The arranger must develop a clear vision of how to make effective use of shapes and forms naturally provided by the materials. As an exercise in composition, imagine how this arrangement would appear if the lower pink chrysanthemum were standing upright, as the *soe* complement. How would this detract from the one-directional movement?

Above: **Nageire: Informal right-hand arrangement, third variation.** Vase: Contemporary Nageire ceramic with skirt, in brown glaze. The branches of quince japonica are placed in a form that has been introduced before and is similar to Niju Ike in Seika (see pages 83–85). Placement of *soe* is 10 degrees to the left and 10 degrees forward. Flowering quince has its own natural curvature, which the artist has utilized very well in this arrangement. The energy of the plant's future growth is suggested. The *shin* flower complement is simply replaced with narcissus leaves, and the *soe* complement flowers of narcissus, as a group, add to the freestyle aspect. On the far lower right, the placement for the *tai* quince branch is 80 degrees to the right and 80 degrees forward. Yellow chrysanthemums serve as *tai* complement flowers and, in addition, cover the rim. Please notice the direction of the narcissus leaves, which enhance the line in the branches. In this type of flower vase, with a narrow base, pebbles are often put in to add weight and to counterbalance the extended branches.

Opposite: **Nageire: Using informal third-variation concepts for a freestyle arrangement.** Vase: Contemporary brown-glazed Nageire ceramic with stem. Camellia branches often have unique shapes in their lines. A first step, when examining a branch, is to determine which lines should be enhanced for *shin* (90 degrees horizontal, 60 degrees forward). (The angle at which this photograph was taken makes *shin* appear to be disproportionately short.) Placement for *soe* is 45 degrees to left and 40 degrees forward. To find this 45-degree angle, draw an imaginary line from the top blossom to the bottom of the branch; that line lies at a 45-degree angle. The beautiful curve of this *soe* branch was not apparent until excess limbs and leaves were removed. Placement for *tai* is 80 degrees right and 70 degrees to the front. Camellia blossoms, in general, fall soon after the blossom is fully opened. Because of this tendency, using camellia blossoms in arrangements is often avoided, especially under certain circumstances. To keep a blossom in place for a period of time, gently open it up, push a straight pin into the center of the blossom, and press down through the receptacle and stem. Because of the many stamens, the pinhead will not show.

Nageire: Informal third-variation freestyle arrangement. Vase: Contemporary white-glazed ceramic. The two pink Scabiosa (also called "pincushion") flowers on the far left function as *shin* in this third-variation arrangement. The raspberry branch on the far right functions as *tai*. The Scabiosa on the right, above the *tai* raspberry branch, functions as *soe*. Once an arranger grasps the basic concept of any of the styles—formal, semiformal, or informal—as well as the use of angles, he or she can improvise and add the necessary materials to complete the arrangement. The raspberry branch hanging down on the left complements the *soe* flowers. The overall impression is almost that the design is radiating from the center. White chrysanthemums and buds of Scabiosa form a mass in the center to anchor the outward movement of the lines. The choice of vase enhances the light-colored floral materials and conveys a happy mood of spring.

Nageire: Freestyle, based upon the informal style. Vase: Contemporary white Nageire ceramic. Japanese witch hazel branches have exciting curves in line that are provided by nature. It is a joy to work with materials that have these inspiring lines and, in addition, are accented with yellow blossoms. The left-hand branch is placed first. To enhance a unique curve in the line, a straight limb was cut short, and the cut section was cleverly hidden by the blossoms. The branches to the left have been skillfully trimmed to provide the artistically desired pattern. On the far left, the tip of the main branch was removed and the cut hidden with flowers. Again, at the sharp curved angle, another cut is concealed by flowers. In Seika, Moribana, and freestyle, the key to the art of arrangement is to carefully study natural materials and determine which elements already present are useful for your design. Decisions must be made on which elements can be used as they are, and which should be twisted, readjusted, or simply eliminated to fit the design. This arrangement with Japanese witch hazel is a very good example of the way an artist's judgment for elimination can enhance the total design. The right-hand branch has been added to provide balance, and purple iris buds serve as contrast to the golden witch hazel blossoms.

The Symbolism of Plants

It should be emphasized here that Western countries, and, indeed, all nations or states, have their own symbolic associations to flowers and plants. They may be related to religion (lily), military distinction (oak-leaf clusters), political achievement (laurel), superstition (four-leaf clover), poetry (rose), and so on. American states have their symbolic flowers (sunflower: Kansas), and many European "dynasties" had theirs (fleur-de-lis: France).

The symbolism of plants in Japan derives from many sources: the age-old association of flowers with ceremonies, Confucian and Buddhist traditions from China, and Japan's own native lore. Like all symbolism, East and West, it is vague and subject to various interpretations, for it is based primarily on analogies or likenesses between an object–in this instance, a plant–and an unseen quality such as courage; a desirable state such as long life and happiness; or a rare person, as tender and beautiful as a flower. The Japanese pink, Dianthus superbus, called *nadeshiko* in Japanese, is one of the plants symbolizing feminine grace, and Japanese women are often called Yamato-Nadeshiko. Similarly, certain irises with tall, straight leaves stand for a promising young boy and are used in arrangements for the Boys' Festival, on the fifth day of the fifth month. Specific flowers are identified with the four seasons and with the festivities associated with the twelve months of the year.

Some plants are male (*yo*)–tall, vigorous flowers, and branches and blossoms of bright colors; others are female (*in*)–trailing, graceful specimens like the willow, and flowers of soft, pastel shades. Certain combinations of plant material are dearly loved, such as the "three friends of winter" (*sho-chiku-bai*) or the "seven grasses of autumn" (*aki no nana gusa*). The "three friends" are pine, bamboo, and plum–or, as variants, plum, green orchid, and chrysanthemum, or bamboo, ardisia (an evergreen with clusters of berries), and club moss. The evergreen character and the strength of pine suggest endurance "even against the winds of adversity," the steadfastness of friends, and long life. The resilience of bamboo, bending with the wind but not breaking, is analogous to pliancy and adaptability; its greenness suggests constancy, and its widespread growth and ample supply of shoots represent abundance and prosperity. First to bloom in the frosty days of early spring, even before its leaves come out, the plum stands for hardiness and courage, and the delicacy of the petals against the brown bark makes it the symbol of sheer loveliness. This combination is appropriate in arrangements for the New Year, for weddings, and for other embarkings on new ventures where good omens and staunch virtues are to be hoped for.

The seven grasses of autumn are native to the hillsides and banks of streams in the Japanese countryside. They are slender, and their flowers, small and muted in color, convey the mood of gentle melancholy characteristic of the season. They are: bush clover, Chinese bellflower, Dianthus superbus, patrinia, kudzu vine, Miscanthus, and thoroughwort.

Plum, bamboo, chrysanthemum, and green orchid with pods–associated with four famous Chinese poets and scholar-recluses–are called "four noble characters" or "four beloved ones" (*shi kunshi*). The flowers of the four seasons are sometimes displayed together with their representation in a painting, or perhaps with a small sculpture of a bird or animal associated with them:

Spring: Peony (moutain, or peach), together with a nightingale
Summer: Lotus, with a duck
Autumn: Chrysanthemum or grasses, with quail or partridge
Winter: Plum, with a magpie

The Japanese flower calendar, as presented here, is not rigid, but this list provides a general picture:

January: Bamboo, narcissus, pine, plum
February: Plum, camellia, adonis, crocus
March: Peach, pussy willow, forsythia, anemone
April: Cherry, apricot, magnolia, primrose
May: Azalea, peony, wisteria, iris
June: Iris, peony, lily, hollyhock
July: Hydrangea, lotus, lily, spirea
August: Morning glory, sunflower, rhododendron, water lily
September: Gourd, seven grasses of autumn, aconite (monkshood), gentian
October: Maple, dahlia, cosmos, canna
November: Chrysanthemum, cockscomb, daisy, bittersweet
December: Nandina domestica (sacred bamboo), holly, Rhodea japonica, poinsettia

The following list will convey some idea of the kinds of connotations that plants may bring to the Japanese mind. In some instances, these will be familiar to the Western reader; in other cases, they will be very different from the Western interpretation. Not every "meaning" is given for every plant, nor can such a list hope to include every variety of plant material in the rich and varied lexicon of Oriental symbolism. Nevertheless, it is hoped that the examples provided and the suggestions for handling and arranging these materials will be helpful to the Western reader who would like to re-create not only the form but the emotional content of Ikebana.

Acacia: *Friendship*
The white and red varieties also symbolize elegance and nobility; the yellow, secret love. It is best to strip most of the leaves from around the blossom, so as to expose the bloom and the lovely line of the stem.

Aconite (monkshood): *Animosity, hostility*
The Japanese name means "bird helmet." Purple aconite is attractive in autumn arrangements when combined with golden leaves.

Adonis (pheasant's eye): *Reminiscence, blessing*
The Japanese name means "happy long-life plant." This flower is used in decorations for the morning of New Year's Day. Flowers and leaves are ideally combined with bare branches in winter.

Agapanthus: *Love letters*
The Japanese name means "purple prince orchid." The showy flowers on their long stems suit agapanthus to the role of shin in Moribana arrangements. Its long leaves, like those of the amaryllis, are the best accompaniment, but other green leaves, or dry materials, are also suitable.

Amaranth cockscomb: *Affected person*
Evergreens add interest to arrangements of amaranth.

Amaryllis: *Attractiveness, pride*
Light-colored amaryllis also symbolize ravishing but affected beauty; dark-colored ones, chattering talk. Only a few blossoms are

needed in an arrangement, and the leaves should be given prominence.

Anemone: *Truth, sincerity*
The red anemone says "I love you"; yellow indicates loneliness, a breaking-off, as of a friendship; purple symbolizes belief, faith. The beautiful long stems of this flower should be utilized in the design of the arrangement.

Apple: *Righteousness, justice, exactitude*
A flowering branch is ideal for arranging. If you use one with a few tiny new apples, the feeling of harvest time and trees burdened with fruit will be enhanced by the bent, arched line of the branch. If other flowers are used with apple blossoms, be careful that they do not destroy each other's beauty.

Apricot: *Doubt, distrust*
The old Japanese name for apricot meant "old Chinese peach flower." In arrangements, flowering branches are best used in combination with several larger flowers and leaves from another kind of plant. Dark red tulips or daffodils with their own leaves are excellent choices.

Aspidistra: *Improving fortunes*
This is the ideal green leaf for use, alone or in combination with almost any flower, in any style of Ikebana.

Aster: *Sentimental recollections*
Use asters in the same way as chrysanthemums, but on a smaller scale. Cut short, they are excellent for hiding the kenzan when used to complement branches.

Azalea: *Temperance, moderation*
The white azalea means "first love," the red one "joy of love." Both flowering branches and foliage alone are excellent material. The lines of the branches of even a short piece look much like a miniature tree and are therefore ideal for creating natural-looking arrangements.

Baby's breath (Gypsophila): *Pure heart*
Not used alone, Gypsophila combines well with almost any material, as a complement, or as shin with one or two bright flowers in a modern design.

Balsam (Impatiens balsamina): *Impatience*
"Touch me not" is the message, and one of the names, of this plant. Pink balsam is also symbolic of a tomboy. The old Japanese name meant "manicure," for the petals of pink-toned varieties were rubbed on the fingernails to color them. In autumn, the fruit

of this plant will pop open and spill its seed if it is touched–thus the name "touch me not." This flower is attractive when combined with narrow branches or tall, slender grasses.

Bamboo: *Steadfastness, pliancy, constancy, abundance*
The prince of grasses. Traditionally used for New Year's arrangements. The bamboo must be heavily trimmed to create the familiar clean, open lines.

Begonia: *Unrequited love*
A representative flower of autumn in Japan, its name means "flower of the autumn sea." A simple Chabana arrangement, contrasting the wide leaf with small pink flowers, is much favored by tea ceremony masters.

Bittersweet: *Truth*
Such wild-growing materials, with beautiful lines and bright berries, are excellent for both naturalistic and abstract arrangements in the modern vein.

Bletilla: *Patience*
Ideal for making small naturalistic arrangements using no other materials. Bletilla leaves combine well with bright flowers or dried vines.

Blueberry: *Prayer*
Excellent for making landscape scenes, because even a small branch has the characteristic bushiness of the whole. The light-green and coppery leaves and the interesting shape of the branches create miniature trees.

Broom: *Tidiness*
There is great beauty in the fine, leafy stems, which are easily bent to form dramatic curves. The Chinese name for these blooms means "golden baby sparrows."

Bulrush: *Loneliness*
Place bulrushes upright and combine them with aquatic or waterside flowers to create a landscape, or bend and tie the stalks to achieve an abstract arrangement.

Burnet: *Prankishness, roguery, mischief*
The old Japanese name referred to a sort of sweet dumpling on a stick, with the same connotations of childhood that lollipops have in the West. The long, hard stems with their small, stiff flowers lend themselves especially to modern arrangements.

Bush clover: *Thoughtful, pensive mood*
One of the seven grasses of autumn. Strip enough flowers and leaves from the branches

so that flowers and bare branches alternate, thus emphasizing the lovely arched line.

Caladium (elephant's ear): *Great joy and delight*
The unusual colors and patterns of these leaves remind the Japanese of rich brocades. They are ideal for modern arrangements, using only a leaf or two with a single brilliantly colored blossom.

Calendula: *Sadness of separation, broken heart, heartache*
These are ideal combined with branches of any kind.

Camellia: *Pride*
The red camellia also symbolizes nobility of reasoning; the white variety, ideal love. Tea ceremony masters like to use single blooms, which can be arranged with great effectiveness and drama. Retain only two or three leaves, to emphasize the beauty of the blossoms and the supple branches.

Canna: *Forever, eternally*
To avoid a heavy look, substitute thin, narrow leaves of other plants, and use the canna leaves with other flowers.

Carnations: *Passion*
White carnations also mean "living for love"; red carnations indicate a less strong passion. Yellow carnations say, "I do not believe you." Ferns or other greenery combine well with these popular flowers.

Castor-oil plant: *Destiny, fortune*
This plant is ideal for arranging in or out of bloom, because the leaves have an interesting hand shape, with red or green-and-red "fingers."

Cattail: *Recovery from illness*
The old Japanese name meant "screen grass," because cattails were used to weave fences. When fresh, they are used for creating naturalistic waterside scenes in large, shallow containers. When dried, especially with their leaves bunched and tied into various shapes, they are used for abstract creations.

Cherry: *Nobility*
The cherry blossom is the national flower of the Japanese people. Flowering cherry branches are so glorious that it is unwise to combine other flowers with them, but they may be used in combination with nonflowering branches, as for example with evergreens.

Chestnut: *Impartiality, fairness*
In autumn, chestnuts appear, and the

branches are lovely to use in arrangements. Retain only a few leaves on each branch, so that its line may be visible and the contrast between leaves and nuts is strengthened.

China aster: *Reverence, cherishing a memory*
Combine China asters with branches of any kind.

Chinese bellflower: *Sadness, despondence*
One of the seven grasses of autumn. The blue and purple tones of this flower, or a white variety, may be combined interestingly with branches of red or gold autumn foliage.

Chloranthus: *Great value*
The old Japanese name referred to a sum of money, in gold coins, which would now be equivalent to a million dollars. One reason for this name is the coral color of the berries—coral was a highly prized rare gem. Chloranthus is widely used for ceremonial New Year's arrangements, looking toward a large fortune in the coming year. It combines well with bare branches, for it has beautiful green leaves in addition to its large, colorful berries.

Chrysanthemum: *Noble simplicity*
The white chrysanthemum is symbolic of a faithful wife; the red says, "I love you." Deep colors say, "Believe me." The yellow varieties indicate vague memories. Avoid using huge blossoms in formal arrangements—they are more beautiful used singly. The leaf is often as important as the bloom, so try to incorporate as many leaves as possible into the design. Use the contrast of slightly opened, half-opened, and fully opened blooms when using the smaller sizes.

Clematis: *Gentle love*
The white clematis means "out of gratitude, to repay." The purple variety means "unchanged, for eternity." The Japanese name means "temple bell" or "lantern flower." Combine with any kind of branch.

Clivia: *Nobility*
This regal flower is best arranged alone, with its own sword-shaped leaves. If it is to be arranged with branches, use it as a complement in a large-scale arrangement.

Clover: *Honest labor*
The three-leaf clover is a symbol of hope, religion, love. The four-leaf clover means love, honor, health, wealth, and good luck in love. Blossoms bunched together and combined with leaves can be arranged in a crystal vase. Vines may be used with clover blooms for line.

Cockscomb: *Grotesque*
Though an autumn flower, cockscomb is not effective used with autumn leaves, because the colors are too similar. Combine with evergreens.

Coleus: *Tragic love*
Coleus leaves are so unusual that it is best to use just one, with a single flower, in a modern container.

Columbine: *Inconstancy, fickleness*
Columbine combines ideally with palm leaves or ferns.

Cosmos: *Pure love of a virgin*
The white cosmos indicates purity and elegance; the red, a warm heart. Use the twisted stems to create interesting modern designs.

Crape myrtle: *Unpreparedness*
The Japanese name, meaning "the monkey slips," refers to the extreme smoothness of the branches. Only used when it is in bloom and covered with brilliant red blossoms, crape myrtle combines best with large white flowers and green leaves.

Crocus: *Joy of youth, pleasure*
The yellow crocus says, "Please believe me," and the blue says, "I believe you, but I am still worried." The red variety says, "You love me so much it worries me," and the purple says, "Maybe I regret my prior love for you." (The white crocus appears to be silent in Japanese flower symbolism.) These small flowers are ideal for creating miniature arrangements.

Cyclamen: *Jealousy, distrust*
White cyclamen indicates a warmhearted person. The light-colored varieties say, "I understand you." Red cyclamen's message is, "I will not economize." This flower is effective when placed in a container that does not show the stems. Use the blossoms grouped in one corner of a modern vase for a contemporary arrangement.

Daffodil: *Unrequited love*
Any green leaves or branches can be used with daffodils, or they can be effectively arranged with their own leaves or with white-painted branches.

Dahlia: *Gratitude*
The white dahlia expresses gratitude to parents. The red dahlia's message is, "You make me happy," while the variegated ones say, "I think of you constantly." Yellow means "I am happy that you love me." When dahlias are combined with branches, small or medium

flowers should be used. If large blooms are to be arranged, put just one in the corner of a modern vase and complement it with ferns or other linear material.

Daisy: *Innocence, fond memories*
The Japanese name means "long-lived chrysanthemum." Daisies are especially useful for covering a kenzan that holds other flowers.

Daphne: *Grandeur, magnificence*
Daphne is best arranged during its flowering season, in naturalistic fashion, with large, smooth-petaled flowers such as tulips.

Delphinium: *Sweetness, beauty*
Use as a complement in Moribana arrangements, with bushy material for the main branches, or with large green leaves in modern arrangements.

Deutzia: *Shyness*
The Japanese name means "hollow tree," a reference to deutzia's hollow stems. They are very popular for arranging because of the clusters of fragrant white flowers and brilliant green leaves. Strip the stems partially to bring out their lines.

Dianthus: *Love*
White dianthus denotes talent, and the red means cheerfulness. The double varieties say, "My love will never die." Variegated blossoms signify talent. Because of its shape and color range, the dianthus is representative of woman. Dianthus is ideally arranged in a natural style, with bushy foliage used to complement the flower.

Dogwood: *Continuity*
The Japanese name means "water wood," because dogwood grows in damp places and requires a large amount of water. Combine flowering branches with any green material, taking care not to hide the smooth lines of the branches.

Enkianthus: *Nobility*
The Japanese name means "star-filled sky," because when it blooms, the whole bush is covered with small white blossoms. Ideal arranging material in spring, summer, and autumn.

Eucalyptus: *Temptation*
The shape, symmetry, and leatherlike texture of the leaves give character and interest to this material. There are several varieties, but the most commonly used is the long-stemmed, large-leafed kind. The stem is easily bent into interesting shapes, but some of the leaves should be removed to stress the line.

Euonymus alata (burning bush): *Pomp, splendor*
The Japanese name means "Chinese brocade tree," referring to its colorful autumn foliage. The bare stems are especially suited to arrangements in the abstract style.

Euonymus japonica: *A long time, but not eternity*
The variegated types, rimmed in yellow or white, are especially useful in Ikebana, particularly Moribana and Nageire styles. They must be heavily stripped before use.

Flameflower (tritoma): *Disbelief*
The long, clean stems with their dramatic flower heads allow flameflowers to play the role of shin very well. Open-petaled flowers, like dahlias or daisies, with their own leaves, provide interesting contrast.

Forget-me-not: *True love*
Use these flowers wired together in bunches and combined with branches.

Forsythia: *Submissiveness, good nature*
The old Japanese name meant "bird's wing," because of the wing-shaped blossoms. The graceful curves of the branches make forsythia an ideal material at any season. Place arrangements so that the branches can droop naturally—hanging from a shelf, for example.

Foxglove (digitalis): *Decision*
Foxglove is attractive combined with large wide leaves or ferns.

Freesia: *Innocence*
Use as *nejime* with any long-stemmed leaves or flowers. Do not combine with bushes. Used alone, it is lovely for modern arrangements.

Gardenia: *Purity*
The gardenia means "I am very happy." Work with buds in arranging; the flowers open very quickly, and the finished arrangement will actually show open flowers. Strip leaves from around the bloom to show the stem line and prevent a heavy, overly full look.

Gentian: *Righteousness, justice*
Use with long leaves in a small Nageire arrangement, or combine with branches and daisies.

Gerbera: *Sadness*
Excellent for modern arrangements, used with its own leaves or others.

Gladiolus: *Secret*
The old Japanese name means "foreign iris." use the leaves as you would the blossoms in arrangements.

Globe amaranth (bachelor's buttons): *Undying love*
The Japanese name means "thousand-day pink," because of its excellent keeping qualities. Interesting arrangements may be made by tying a number of blossoms in a bunch and setting them in a contemporary vase. Any type of green may be combined with these flowers.

Gloxinia: *Coquetry, flirtation*
Gloxinia blossoms have a velvety texture that makes them very effective used singly in a tall slender crystal vase, in combination with several long, slender leaves.

Hawthorn: *Waiting for success*
In Japan, the fruit of the hawthorn is added to fish as it cooks, to soften the bones and make them edible. Very beautiful in arrangements, it is necessary to strip off most of the leaves to reveal the beauty of the blossoms.

Hibiscus: *Fragile beauty*
The Japanese call hibiscus the "drunk lady flower" because it is white when it first blooms and then turns pink. It is best arranged alone, using buds and only one or two open blossoms.

Hollyhock: *Simplicity, peace*
The white hollyhock also symbolizes a pure heart, and the pink variety, true love. Both the flower and leaf of this plant are attractive, but the stem is large and straight and is best augmented with intertwining vines.

Hosta: *Devotion*
Use in small-scale naturalistic arrangements, with its own leaves. These leaves are also very interesting combined with other flowers.

Hydrangea: *Conceit*
White hydrangea also symbolizes a wanderer. Avoid using more than a few open blooms. Rather, contrast full and partly open blossoms with a few buds, to prevent an overly heavy look.

Iris ensata (Japanese Iris): *Elegant spirit*
One of the traditional flowers for Boys' Day in Japan. The shape of the narrow leaves is very much like that of a Japanese sword, thus symbolizing courage. The tall, straight stems stand for straightforwardness, and the purple or white flowers for nobility. Use a shallow dish and stones to re-create their natural waterside setting.

Iris laevigata (Rabbit-ear iris): *Good fortune*
The traditional Japanese flower of the early summer season. Arrange like other iris.

Iris sanguinea (Siberian flag): *Messenger*
The Siberian flag is considered to be feminine, just as the Japanese iris is masculine. Although it grows in dry soil, it can be used interchangeably with other irises.

Iris tectorum: *Correspondence*
This plant is native to China, and there is an old Chinese superstition that if it is planted on the straw roofs of barns, the farm will be safe from typhoons. The old Japanese name means "safety for children," an obvious derivation from the old Chinese tale. Use the leaves as abundantly as the blooms in an arrangement.

Ivy: *Friendship, marriage*
Ivy is attractive used in hanging arrangements, or entwined around a piece of weathered wood. Ivy combines beautifully with small white flowers of the chrysanthemum type.

Job's-tears: *Unity*
Combine with waterside plants in a large, shallow container to create a landscape. Or use only the stems with their clusters of seeds to create an abstract arrangement in autumn.

Kerria japonica: *Noble spirit*
Autumn, when the vine is in flower, is the ideal time to use kerria. Use a large, shallow bowl filled with water, so that the reflection of the lovely arch of the vine may be enjoyed.

Kudzu vine: *Recovery from illness*
One of the seven grasses of autumn. The leaves, large, smooth, and almost round, are very interesting combined with many flowers other than their own.

Laurel: *Victory, honor*
Use laurel with stock or similar flowers.

Lilac: *First love, friendship*
When using lilacs in arrangements, add green leaves as complement, and perhaps a few smooth-petaled flowers such as tulips.

Lily: *Purity*
The many varieties of lilies are all ideal for arranging. The blossoms usually grow facing outward rather than upward, so try to use blooms that have no tendency to droop.

Lily of the valley: *Returning happiness*
Arrange the leaves in an interesting design, using a small kenzan to secure them. Only a few blossoms are needed to complete the picture, which can be very effectively presented in a crystal champagne goblet.

Loosestrife: *Wishes granted*
The Japanese name means "tiger's tail," a reference to the shape of the blossoms. Arrange in natural style, using almost any kind of branches.

Lotus: *Pure love*
Ceremonial arrangements for Buddhist temples very often used the lotus flower and leaf. The interesting shape of the seed pod makes it an excellent material for contemporary arrangements.

Lupine: *Avarice*
The Japanese name means "upright wisteria." Combine it with vines, ferns, or any green materials.

Lycoris: *Temptation*
These brilliant red, flamelike flowers are often found in graveyards. Parents warn their children not to pick them or to bring them into the house, for fear the house will catch fire, bringing certain death to the family. Such tales prevent most children from handling these flowers, whose roots contain a very strong poison. Because of this legend, lycoris is only used in modern arrangements.

Magnolia grandiflora: True, sincere love
Bloom and leaves are so large that this flower is best used for large-scale arrangements. Otherwise, use only one blossom and remove most of the leaves.

Magnolia liliiflora: *Love of nature*
Excellent for Nageire-style arrangements. This variety produces its blooms before its leaves, so other green leaves must be added.

Maple: *Neatness*
Excellent Moribana and Nageire material, from spring through autumn. The leaves must be carefully stripped to bring out the lines of the branches. Almost any flowers go well with maple.

Marigold: *Health*
The Japanese name means "thousand-happiness chrysanthemums." A most versatile plant, it can be combined with almost any material in almost any style.

Marvel-of-Peru (four-o'clock): *Diffidence, bashfulness*
The Japanese name for this flower means "face powder," for a fine powder may be found inside the fruit. The leaves are as lovely as the blossoms, so this flower is ideal in combination with bare branches.

Miscanthus: *Sorrow*
One of the seven grasses of autumn. In the summer, before the ears form, the tall, slender leaves are very handsome and useful for arrangements in any style, even the abstract. In the autumn, bunch the ears to make modern arrangements.

Morning glory: *Attachment, mortal love*
The blossoms do not last very long, but cutting them early, before the dew had left them, prolongs their life. It is best to use only one or two blossoms, combined with the interesting lines of their vines.

Nandina domestica: *Domestic assistance*
Known as the "sacred bamboo," although it does not belong to the bamboo family. Nandina, which bears red or white berries, is used in arrangements for festive occasions, and traditionally a spray of leaves and a bunch of berries are laid on top of a gift of food to attest to its purity. Nandina is not arranged when it is in flower.

Narcissus: *Self-love*
White narcissus also means "veiled in mystery"; variegated kinds indicate unrequited love. Yellow ones say, "Please take my love." Summer narcissus indicate satisfaction or gratification of lust. Often used in traditional flower arrangements, the beautiful leaves are sometimes more important than the blossoms. Narcissus combine wonderfully with evergreens.

Nasturtium: *Victory*
The Japanese name means "golden water lily," because the leaves are so similar. Arrange with their own leaves in small-scale modern arrangements.

Oak: *Prosperity*
Especially suitable for arrangements in autumn. Chrysanthemums, especially medium-sized white ones, are the perfect complement.

Ornamental onion flowers: *Patience*
One of the recent additions to the list of Ikebana materials, onion flowers, with their smooth, irregularly curving stems and thistlelike heads, appeal to the modern arranger.

Pansy: *Friendship*
The message of the pansy is "Think of me." White pansies stand for elegance and gentleness, purple ones symbolize honesty and faithfulness, and yellow ones indicate a small happiness. They really need no definite arrangement to enhance their colorful beauty,

but they may be tied into a bunch and set into a modern vase with none of the stems showing. Or they may be combined with branches or dried materials.

Patrinia: *Thoughtfulness*
One of Japan's seven grasses of autumn. The Japanese consider patrinia to be especially feminine, because of its slender, delicate form. Combine the tall stems of this flower with slender grasses for an elegant arrangement. Or take the blooms from the stems and wire them in a bunch at the base of the stems as a focal point.

Paulownia: *Nobility*
The emblem of the empress of Japan, and the informal emblem of the royal family. Use flower-bearing branches in naturalistic arrangements, and seed-bearing branches, with their dramatic, velvety golden berries, in more abstract ones.

Peach: *Domesticity, congeniality*
The peach blossom says, "You stole my heart." This is one of the traditional flowers for Girls' Day in Japan and is associated with femininity in the same way that plum branches are associated with masculinity. Peach branches should not be bent or manipulated—this material should be used in as natural a way as possible. It combines well with evergreens and with small-petaled flowers such as stock or candytuft and their leaves.

Peony: *Shyness*
In China, peonies are considered to be the king of all flowers, and they are also very popular in Japan. The tree peony and the regular peony belong to the same family and are so similar that they are known as the "twin sister flowers." When arranging either sort, use only one fully open blossom. Fill in with buds and half-open blooms. No other material is needed.

Petunia: *Idealism*
Combine with branches, or with long green leaves, like those of the phoenix.

Phlox: *Coquetry*
Use this charming flower to complement branches in Moribana arrangements, or mass the flower heads and rest them in the mouth of a dramatic container.

Phoenix palm: *Sentimental recollections*
Any feathery leaves of this type are ideal for the contemporary styles of arrangement, combined with any flower. They lend themselves to trimming and reshaping for dramatic effects in the abstract manner.

Pine: *Happiness and long life, endurance*
The king of trees, pine is used in Japan on festive occasions. A traditional New Year's combination, called "the three friends of winter," may consist of pine, bamboo, and flowering plum.

Pitcher plant (Nepenthes): *Danger*
This insectivorous plant is used only for arrangements in the abstract style. Combine with dried materials or anthurium in striking modern containers.

Plum: *Courage, hardiness, loveliness*
Plum is associated with the masculine, and with nobility and purity. In arrangements, it is ideally combined with pine. Straight young flowering branches may be used with large-petaled flowers such as tulips.

Poinsettia: *Joy*
Combine with evergreens or with white-painted branches in a contemporary style. Use only one or two blossoms.

Pomegranate blossoms: *Lovers*
The brilliant orange blossoms and green leaves contrast beautifully in arrangements. In autumn, when the fruit appears, interestingly shaped branches are effective. Many of the leaves should be stripped to allow the lines to contrast with the fruit. White chrysanthemums or daisies are lovely complements.

Poppy: *Rest*
The white poppy indicates sleep, and the pink indicates solace. Orange poppies symbolize vanity, and deep-red ones, enthusiasm. Not often used in classical styles, they are ideal for modern arrangements.

Portulaca: *Unrequited love*
The Japanese name means "pine-needle peony," because the shapes are so similar. Try wiring the blooms together to give them weight, and then sinking them into a crystal bowl, allowing the blooms to float rather than rest against the mouth of the bowl.

Primrose: *Hope*
The white primrose means "charming, lovely"; red indicates a quest for fortune; purple indicates authenticity and reliability. These small flowers are best arranged by tying them into bunches and resting the bunches against the mouth of a vase.

Pussy willow: *Recovery from illness*
Early opening of the bud may be induced by peeling back its skin. By forcing open only a few buds, a lovely contrast between the silver of the open ones and the red of the unopened ones is produced.

Quince: *Triteness, mediocrity, the commonplace*
The only reasonable explanation for this inappropriate symbolism would seem to be that quince blooms at almost any season and in every kind of weather, in Japan. But the old Japanese name meant "wood melon," because of the melonlike shape of the buds, and this name was corrupted to the word for "fool." Quince is the most perfect material for any style of Ikebana. It can be bent to any shape, the blossoms will last for two or three days even without water, and the dramatic angles of even bare branches lend themselves to arranging.

Reed: *Anxiety, music*
Reeds are ideally arranged in a long, shallow bowl, their height used as a background for iris or lilies cut shorter.

Rhodea: *Eternal youth*
The Japanese name means "ten-thousand-year green." Often arranged in Seika style for happy occasions. Or use a few leaves, combined with one bright flower, in an unusual vase.

Rhododendron: *Devotion, brotherly love*
The beautiful shape and color of both leaf and blossom make the rhododendron ideal for arranging. Try to use more buds than fully opened flowers, and strip off quite a few leaves to allow the interesting line of the branch to show. Several leaves should be removed from around the blooms to eliminate the formal, symmetrical look.

Rose: *Love, beauty*
The white rose symbolizes love and respect, the yellow rose, jealousy and stagnant love. Pink stands for a beautiful girl, and deep-pink ones indicate shyness. The red double rose is a symbol of harmony. Single-petaled varieties mean "simple, uncomplicated," and dead-white roses mean "promise for a whole life." White buds symbolize delicacy, red ones, innocent hope. Rose thorns mean relief that a misfortune did not turn into tragedy. The rose is beautiful arranged in any manner.

Salvia: *A lovely heart*
This brilliantly colored flower is effective when used with highly colored leaves or in a bright vase, to create a very modern small arrangement.

Sedum: *Restfulness*
The thick, waxy leaves are interesting in modern arrangements. In the fall flowering season, combine with autumn foliage.

Silk tree: *Vainglory, vanity, ostentation*
The Japanese name means "sleeping tree," because the leaves fold up at dusk. Gently curving branches lend themselves to Nageire arrangements. The leaves combine well with other flowers.

Smilax: *Memory of love*
The long thorny branches and handsome clusters of green berries make smilax an ideal material for Nageire or modern arrangements. The leaves combine well with other flowers.

Snapdragon: *Haughtiness, arrogance*
The Japanese name means "golden fish flower." A very versatile material, snapdragons may be combined with any leaves or branches, but should be the only kind of flower in an arrangement.

Sorbus: *Caution, prudence*
Summer, when it bears clusters of white flowers, and autumn, when it turns color, are the best seasons for arranging sorbus. Moribana, Nageire, and naturalistic modern arrangements are best.

Spirea: *Victory*
The Japanese name means "snow-covered willow." the beautiful white-flowered arcs are ideal material for arranging, especially when the branches still have a few unopened buds as well as open blossoms. Autumn, when the leaves begin to turn, is also an excellent time to use spirea.

Stock: *Beauty of eternity*
Arrange with any green material, especially phoenix, but do not combine with other flowers.

Sunflower: *Respect*
The Japanese name means "turning with the sun." Contemporary and abstract styles are best. The dried seed pods are often used in abstract creations. Do not combine sunflowers with other blossoms.

Sweet pea: *Tender memory*
Several sweet peas wired together will stand securely in a kenzan. Several such bunches may then be combined with ferns or other interesting greenery.

Thistle: *Independence, dignity, vengeance*
The leaves and stems of most thistles are unattractive. Mass the blossoms and use them with large, smooth leaves, like those of the monstera (split-leaf philodendron).

Thoroughwort: *Hesitation, indecision, scruples*
One of the seven grasses of autumn. Long, slender green leaves are especially effective with thoroughwort, but any branches combine well with it, too.

Tuberose: *Dangerous love*
Tuberoses may grow to a height of three feet and are excellent for tall, slender arrangements. The stem, which is uninteresting, may be covered with the leaves of another flower.

Tulip: *Charity, benevolence, kindness*
The white tulip also symbolizes lost love; yellow, hopeless love; red, a confession of love; purple, immortal love. Variegated tulips mean "beautiful eyes." Ideal for flower arrangements, the tulip may be combined effectively with many materials and is especially lovely used in combination with branches.

Water lily: *Purity of heart*
The blossom opens in the daytime and closes in the evening; thus, the Japanese name means "sleeping flower." Water lilies are best arranged by floating several blooms in a shallow bowl, thus re-creating their natural setting. Such an arrangement is cool and summery, ideal for hot summer weather.

Weeping willow: *Grace*
Weeping willow can be used to great effect at all times of the year and combines well with almost any kind of material.

Wisteria: *Welcome*
Arrange wisteria in a tall vase, in Nageire style, with its own vines and leaves. The dried vines are attractive for abstract arrangements in the modern style.

Zinnia: *Remembrance of an old friend*
Zinnias bloom through the summer and early autumn, so the Japanese call them "hundred-day flowers." Ideal for summery arrangements, they combine well with any kind of branch.

Plant List

TREES AND BUSHES

Azalea species
Bamboo species
Camellia species
Chinese hawthorn (*kanamemochi*)
Chloranthus glaber (*senryo*)
Cypress species; variegated chaemeocypress, other species
Dogwood (Japanese species)
Eucalyptus species
Euonymus japonica and other species
Forsythia branches and flowers
Ilex holly
Japanese apricot (*ume*, formerly called Japanese plum)
Japanese cherry, many varieties
Juniper species
Maple, various species
Mimosa acacia
Nandina species
Pine: long needles
Pine: short needles, many varieties
Podocarpus: Japanese yew
Quince japonica
Raspberry
Scotch broom
Scotch broom, fasciated
Solanum species, such as bittersweet
Spirea species, both branches and flowers (Japanese dropwort)
Summer sumac
Viburnum (in Japanese, *kinbademari*)
Willow: corkscrew
Willow: fasciated
Willow: weeping
Witch hazel, genus *Hamamelis* (Japanese species, *mansaku*)

FORBS/HERBS

Aspidistra
Anemone
Balloon flower (Chinese bell flower and Turkish balloon flower)
Bulrush species
Calla lily species
Camellia, many varieties
Centaurea (e.g., bachelor's buttons)
Chrysanthemum, many varieties
Convolvulus
Cosmos
Coxcomb species
Cucumber
Daffodils
Delphiniums
Deutzia (Saxifragaceae)
Dianthus (fringed pinks)
Dietes (iris family)
Equisetum (horsetails)
Freesia species
Gayfeathers (*Liatris spicata*)
Gentians (many varieties)
Gerbera species
Heliconia (lobster claw)
Hosta
Hydrangea
Hypericum (St. John's wort)
Iris kakitsubata (Siberian iris)
Iris (*shobu*)
Larkspur
Libertia
Lily (calla)
Lily, variety of species
Lily, pond (*Nuphar polysepalum*; in Japanese, *kohone*)
Lily, toad (*Trycyrtis*; in Japanese, *hototogisu*)
Magnolia species
Millet
Miscanthus species (eulalia; in Japanese, *susuki*)
Narcissus (Japanese species)
New Zealand flax
Peony
Poppy species
Rice plant in early "flower"
Rose species
Scabiosa (pincushion flower)
Statice (*Limonia* species)
Wild poke, pokeweed (*Phytolacca*)
Wisteria
Yellow patrinia

Acknowledgments

Once again I wish to express my great indebtedness to Mr. Kasen Yoshimura, grandmaster of the Ryusei School of Ikebana, in Tokyo, who played a crucial role in the publication of this book, just as he did in the early 1960s, when he supported the publication of my first book on Ikebana, *The Art of Arranging Flowers*. Mr. Kashu Yoshimura, junior grandmaster of the Ryusei School, and the talented professors at the school also deserve my sincere thanks for their support and assistance. Many of the professors at the Ryusei School who provided arrangements for my first book on Ikebana have passed away, but their talents are carried forward by a number of their direct descendents and students who created the arrangements illustrated in this book.

Chief editor Reikiya Imai and his staff at the school's monthly magazine, *Ikebana Ryusei*, unstintingly gave their time and effort to research and prepare the photographs of the flower arrangements for this book. I offer my sincere appreciation. Mr. Tokio Yamanouchi, a well-known documentary film producer and folk-art researcher, and my classmate in college, provided important photographs of a tokonoma in the home of a well-known family in Japan.

I greatly appreciate and thank the Tuttle Publishing Company for producing this book—in particular, publishing director Edward Walters, senior editor Holly Jennings, and former acquisitions editor Jennifer Brown. Finally, I wish to thank my wife, Alice Ogura Sato, who has given me continual support and spent many hours editing the manuscript. I take this opportunity to give my sincere thanks and appreciation to all who have assisted and supported me in this project.

List of Contributing Artists

Author's Note: Many of the arrangements photographed and reproduced in this book were prepared for exhibitions held in locations across Japan; others were made especially for this book by the professors and artists of the Ryusei School.

Third-Generation Grandmaster Kasen Yoshimura
Junior Grandmaster Kashu Yoshimura
Kau'n Ando
Kasui Chiba
Ryofu Fuku
Michihiko Goto
Meiho Hagiwara
Shogetsu Hayashi
Jun'yo Honma
Seiha Iida
Jusui Imano
Keifu Inoue
Tekisui Ishikawa
Kako Ito
Kunsen Kanbayashi
Kaetsu Kimijima

Shiroaki Kimura
Hosen Kobuyama
Ryusen Kobuyama
Shuko Koizumi
Keifu Kumazawa
Senka Kumazawa
Sosen Kurita
Kofu Maruyama
Kosen Matsukawa
Kako Matsuoka
Kogiku Matsuzaka
Satoko Michimukai
Koun Nagahara
Hyakusui Nakata
Shosui Okigami
Shukuho Okutomi
Seigetsu Omori

Kinpu Osaki
Kosen Otsubo
Hou'n Sato (Shozo)
Kiyoto Sekimoto
Seiju Sekimoto
Yofu Sekimoto
Ryuju Shibuyu
Jurin Shono
Gakusen Suzuki
Bien Tabata
Bisho Takeuchi
Eiraku Tanoue
Kikka Yamamoto
Seishu Yamamoto
Zuika Yamamoto
Ryokko Yasukawa

RESOURCE GUIDE

The Ikebana International organization is an excellent source for learning about Ikebana events, exhibitions, and different Ikebana schools. To find out if there is a chapter in your vicinity visit their website (www.ikebanahq.org). Experienced members of a local chapter will be able to guide you to good sources for tools and supplies in your area. If there isn't an Ikebana International chapter near you, try a local garden club. For tools and supplies, you might also check:

• Gift shops that sell Japanese wares
• Local florists

• Craft and hobby shops
• Hardware stores

• Local potters, for ceramic vases

Here is a list of some online stores that offer different kinds of ikebana tools and supplies, including vases and various types of containers, and other Ikebana books.

www.japanese-gardening.com
www.stonelantern.com

www.samadhi-japanese-arts.com
www.chopa.com

Index

The Tuttle Story: "Books to Span the East and West"

Most people are surprised to learn that the world's largest publisher of books on Asia had its humble beginnings in the tiny American state of Vermont. The company's founder, Charles E. Tuttle, belonged to a New England family steeped in publishing. And his first love was naturally books—especially old and rare editions.

Immediately after WW II, serving in Tokyo under General Douglas MacArthur, Tuttle was tasked with reviving the Japanese publishing industry. He later founded the Charles E. Tuttle Publishing Company, which thrives today as one of the world's leading independent publishers.

Though a westerner, Tuttle was hugely instrumental in bringing a knowledge of Japan and Asia to a world hungry for information about the East. By the time of his death in 1993, Tuttle had published over 6,000 books on Asian culture, history and art—a legacy honored by the Japanese emperor with the "Order of the Sacred Treasure," the highest tribute Japan can bestow upon a non-Japanese.

With a backlist of 1,500 titles, Tuttle Publishing is more active today than at any time in its past—inspired by Charles Tuttle's core mission to publish fine books to span the East and West and provide a greater understanding of each.